Well That Explains It:
A Compilation of Researched, Personal Essays

by Marie Shanley

Published by
Marie Shanley / Mxiety

All rights reserved

Copyright © 2020 by Mxiety/Marie Shanley

No part of this book may be reproduced or transmitted in any form or by any means, electronic or mechanical, including photocopying, recording, or by any information storage or retrieval system, permitted by law. For information contact Marie Shanley.

Cover design by Aaron Smith

To my husband, Patrick.
Thank you for always believing I could.

To my sister, Anna Kyra.
Thank you for never telling me I couldn't.

Contents

A Short Intro..11

To Those Who Don't 'Get' Anxiety and Depression, Welcome to My Morning 13

Learning To Be More Comfortable With Needing Antidepressants 19

How My Anxiety & Depression Pushed Me To Grab The Megaphone...23

Things You Do After Growing Up With Narcissistic Parents 27

The Discussions We Should Be Having About Weight Loss 33

How My Eating Disorder Started and Where It Ended.......39

The Importance of Combating PTSD Socially 47

What I Learned About Forgiveness Through My Abusive Parents...53

A Disney Princess Inspired Me to Leave My Abusive Family 59

The Love and Life I Would Have Missed 67

If I had Committed Suicide 67

I'm Not Okay and That's Not Okay...73

3 Reasons Friendships with People Who Have Depression Are Incredible 77

What Being Inside a Flashback Is Like for Someone With PTSD..81

I Can't 'Snap Out' of Depression, but I'm Working on What I Can Control 85

Why Does Social Media Upset Us and What Can We Do? . 89

How I Stopped Comparing Myself to Others and Decided I Was Good Enough 93

The Reality of Loving Someone with Mental Illness 97

How "Kingdom Hearts" Helped Me Through Mental Illness 101

A Year of Following My Purpose; AKA, You Are Not Alone When You're Live 107

Science Reminds Me I Am Small, But I Need To 'Think Big' 111

Following Your Dreams Won't Fix Everything, but Accepting Them Will 115

How Comparing Yourself to Others Is Worse Than Being Depressed 119

How Accepting My Mental Illness Changed My Life 125

Letter to Myself 10 Years Ago 129

What My Childhood Diary Taught Me About Having A Mental Illness 135

Giving Myself Permission to Feel Better 139

What They're Really Saying When They Call You 'Sensitive' 145

Why You Should Be Your Own Friend 151

Mistakes I Have Made While Trying To Help Friends Who Needed Me 157

Am I Afraid Of The Dark? 161

How to Finally 'Take The Leap' In Three Steps 165
A Letter to My Depression 169
Why I Continue Fighting Having Mental Illness 171
What It Costs To Have Anxiety 175
21 Rejections 179
The Beauty of Every Moment of Recovery from Depression
 183
The Bastardization Of Positive Psychology: Recasting negative experiences isn't the same thing as blind optimism
 185
Writer's block. Mental block. 189
Exclusive Essay for *Well That Explains It* 193
Bonus Memoir Preview 199
Thanks 205

A Short Intro

MEMORIES POP INTO MY MIND uninvited quite often. I consider it a side-effect of living with untreated post-traumatic stress disorder for as long as I did. It occurred to me to write them down and share them sometime in 2014. At the time, I was so insecure in my writing (and a bit rightly so, because holy spelling Batman) that I promoted my then-website in no way whatsoever. I was terrified to get on twitter and kind of secretly hoped that no one would actually see what I wrote. Internally, this gave me a green card to continue beating myself up—*woe is me, I am not doing anything to help myself and I'm not magically successful* kind of set up. It's the complicated arena of *I need attention* but being terrified of what I will do when I receive it.

At any rate, as I was reading through the essays, a few things became abundantly clear. First, just because you don't have a reason to do something doesn't mean you shouldn't do it. Because I had no clue why I ever wrote anything, other than because I wanted to write. I didn't think those words would affect me in any way, I just enjoyed getting my thoughts out of my head.

Second, that we are complicated beings, yes, but so much information is out there to explain our complexities. So, I started to add information I found helpful in explaining the world to myself, and suddenly, it was more than just my story.

When I finally put my words out there, I was blown away by the response. The more I wrote, the more people would reach out to me to let me know my words struck them. They too, have been in similar situations and were relieved to know that they are not alone. I hope as you read, you might find some answers for yourself about yourself too.

Finding peace knowing that you are, most certainly, not alone.

To Those Who Don't 'Get' Anxiety and Depression, Welcome to My Morning

WELCOME TO MY MORNING.

I have woken up. I can feel my palms starting to sweat. There's a strong possibility that means a panic attack is coming on.

I take a second to be grateful I didn't wake up from having one because that feels like waking up from drowning. I have a chance to actively fight the thoughts that make me believe I might be dying.

It's time to focus on techniques that get me out of this mindset. I look around my room. I think of how my sheets feel under my back. I can see the sun shining through the window. I can smell my husband's hair on the pillow by mine. I see my dog curled up by the bed. I haven't been conscious for a whole minute, but I have already engaged all of my senses to remind my brain that no, there is no impending attack. I'm okay. I'm safe.

To anyone who has told me I would feel better if I was just more positive, those who say people who need medication are lazy scum. To the anonymous helper who advised that if I just focused on being in balance, all of my issues will go away. And of course, the kind soul who implied this is all for attention — I am dedicating this description of my day to you. As someone who believes we learn better when we are given information and asked to draw our own conclusions, I would like to offer insight into what I have to deal with, instead of just advising that assumptions are usually incorrect.

To wake up and have a chance at a productive day, I need to think of every inch of my body. If I don't do that my brain runs haywire and might decide at any moment that I don't have enough air to breathe.

But hey, I could just smile, right?

The anxious feeling has not subsided. I move to the ground and distract myself. I step onto the floor. Except I cannot just step on it. I need to ask myself, what does the floor feel like? It's cold, but clean. Aware, I realize I kicked off one sock while asleep as I feel the soft cotton on only one foot and the cold hardwood under the other.

As I walk over to the bathroom, I can't make sense of my thoughts. Am I happy? Sad? I focus on untangling them and come to terms with the fact that today will be another day where my head is full. I am already tired of thinking and only five minutes have passed since I opened my eyes.

OK, I think, I wanted to sit down and write again today. I love doing that. But now my mind has moved to remind me how terrible of a writer I am. I know because my mother told me so when I was eight. I can recall every single detail of her facial features as she said that to me. I can feel the paper hitting my feet as she throws the notebook back at me.

Somehow, I am brought back to the present and realize I have made it to the bathroom. I quickly turn on the light. Since I am aware I was just in a flashback, I use the sudden bright light to help me stay present so that I don't get lost in the rest of that memory. It's just a memory, but since I have so many thoughts moving in my mind, it's hard to tell. I don't have time to really acknowledge any of them, but the conclusion I choose to focus on is that I am safe again.

I grab my toothbrush and brush my teeth while walking around getting ready. I'm putting together my to-do list at the same time. Except it's not clear what order things are in. I need to write them down. I start feeling a bit frantic. I *need* to write them down right now. If I don't write them down I will forget and not do anything which means my day will be worth nothing. I growl as I shuffle past my dog, who just wants a morning greeting. He's by my side as I rush into our office with a mouth full of toothpaste to get a piece of paper to write down the list.

Except I already forgot everything I wanted to write. I am forgetful like that. Because I am just a lazy asshole who doesn't want to do anything, so I must be sabotaging myself to make sure I stay a lazy asshole.

Wait, I remind myself, *breathe.*

Or is it because so much is going on, I simply don't have enough short-term memory. I read it's normal for that to happen. No, I know it's because I am garbage. I catch the thought again and feel pain as I understand how I really do believe it. It takes so much out of me to consider this isn't the case. I recall what my therapist and I have discussed to do when this happens, but still cannot remember what it is I wanted to do before I walked into the room.

I hear my husband get up. He walks in on me in the office, holding a toothbrush between my teeth, mouth foaming, pen in hand, frozen over a piece of paper. He asks if I am OK. "I'm trying to remember something," I grumble. Great, now I must also sound like a jerk first thing in the morning. No wonder he'll likely leave me in five years for someone nicer. No, of course he didn't say that to me. He never would. He's a very sweet, kind guy. I have just decided he will. Same way I am sure that I am garbage and that I am lazy.

Giving up on remembering my intention, I walk back into the bathroom. I can't remember if I actually brushed my teeth, so I start over. Finally, I walk over into my closet trying to make up the time I lost as I race against my mind to accomplish *anything*. Anything at all.

That's OK, I remind myself. I am on my hardwood floor, the air is cool around me, the sun is bright out the window. All senses are engaged again in order to re-ground and restart. I start getting dressed. I go back into the bathroom to get my deodorant. I try to recall if I brushed my teeth this time or if I was just holding the brush in my mouth again. I commit to staying in the bathroom for a few more minutes to finally finish the task. I breathe in. I try to recall my to-do list.

I keep an outline of a schedule for every day of the week that I fill in as I go. It says today is social media focused, which I am not good at. I will need to do research, which I enjoy, but I am sure I will miss something important and everyone will finally know how much of a fraud I am. Also, the bathroom needs to be cleaned. It's been a few weeks since I did it last. I remind myself that a good wife would clean her bathroom regularly, so it's another thing I should be better about.

OK, I write down: Bathroom, Social Media, Research, *probably not* Writing. Then what? Hopefully I have a doctor's appointment. I will have to check my phone. A decent person would go to an office job, but I can't seem to get past a second interview. Five recollections flash in my mind at once, two job interviews and two jobs I have had to leave due to panic attacks in the middle of work.

No Marie, there were also toxic people working there, you didn't leave because you couldn't do something or were broken or weak. That leads me to my grounding mantra for today: "I am OK, I am worthy of my own love." I don't believe it, but I have to keep repeating it, because on some days faking it 'til I make it works.

I am finally done brushing my teeth.

Let me think of that same morning, but this time focusing only on being positive... Hmm, it appears that would be exactly the same, except I would also be beating myself up for not being happy, for having failed at thinking all those positive things about myself.

Yes. Everything is a battle in my mind. Everything. Some days the bad thoughts either just don't come in, or they are just not intrusive enough that I have to fight them. On those days I do seem very positive, because my mind isn't spinning faster than I can acknowledge it. This is who I am, and sometimes an easy answer just doesn't work, no matter how badly I want to believe in it.

Some days I wake up and realize I have already lost. The first thing on my mind is how much of a s**t I am and that I don't deserve to waste any space. I look over at my husband and think about how he's stayed with me out of pity. I look at my dog and think about how he only likes me because I feed him.

I don't ask for anyone to feel bad. Indeed, I would prefer not to be treated like a fragile vase. I just ask those who have not walked in another person's shoes, and that's all of us, to avoid assumptions. You don't have to agree with everyone you meet, but you will do much better to assume the best in others instead of the worst. What if they don't disappoint you?

Learning To Be More Comfortable With Needing Antidepressants

THERE IS THIS SOCIAL NOTION that **self-help** is sucking up your emotions and putting them aside to get what you need done. While this may help some people get through a day, in my experience, it has not been the best tool for the long run.

I propose (and this is no novel concept[1]) that we reconsider **self-help** to mean: knowing one's own limits and accepting outside tools and assistance when needed.

I cannot count the number of people I have found on the internet who claim to have medication-free cures, got better by just eating right, exercising, talking to their pastor. You name it, someone has written a way to get around mental illness without having to do the dreaded taboo — take a pill.[2]

Put Down the Pitchforks
I am not here to claim that none of those things work. I am also not here to argue that pharmaceutical companies (and even some bad doctors) aren't trying to push people to take pills they don't need, just to continue making a profit. Taking a non-medicinal approach definitely works[3] for some people. What scares me more is when those who need to take medication to lead more fulfilling lives, avoid it out of fear of crossing social norms.

Whatever the definition of fulfilling is to you, I am sure we can all agree that it does not involve making decisions based on what someone else thinks you should do.

---

[1] *https://www.ncbi.nlm.nih.gov/pmc/articles/PMC1681955/*
[2] *https://www.mhanational.org/medication*
[3] *https://www.psychologytoday.com/us/blog/diagnosis-diet/201709/low-carbohydrate-diet-superior-antipsychotic-medications*

The fear of that judgment is the reason I still don't take ibuprofen[4] until a headache is making my eyes water. Only when it's so bad that I can no longer keep my eyes open in bright light, will I give myself permission to take medicine. It's as though I need to suffer a certain amount before I am *allowed* relief. It's the good ol' belief, that if it's *not obvious or visible, it must not be that bad*. A mentality that has never worked in any scenario (See: Global Warming[5]). Imagine how many ruined days I could avoid if I just took the Tylenol and took care of the problem in its early stages?

I hope one day there will be more than two categories to put people who take medication in. Not just "pill-popper" or "whoops someone didn't take their meds this morning". It should not be that needing or not needing something to function equates to living healthier. Or that being mentally ill makes you an a*hole unless you're medicated.

When did I internalize this?
I was diagnosed with asthma my junior year of high school. My parents were there with me at the doctor's office when I received my prescription, yet when I would administer my inhaler at home, they couldn't help but tell me: "you should really try and see if you can breathe without that thing." I can only imagine what they would have said had they known that the real culprit was anxiety. And yes, to clarify, I could not "breathe without that thing," because anxiety-induced-asthma[6] is also still very real. I spent the next five years with that inhaler, until I tried medication for anxiety and immediately no longer needed it. It wasn't until an ENT doctor suggested that I look into it, that I even considered the anxiety to be related to my breathing. The idea of replacing

---

[4] *https://www.drugs.com/ibuprofen.html*
[5] *https://climate.nasa.gov/evidence/*
[6] *https://asthma.net/living/anxiety-and-asthma-whats-the-deal/*

my inhaler with something for anxiety seemed so audacious at the time. And even more stigmatic than carrying the little red canister with me.

We Can Internalize Better Lessons
There are a few celebrities who talk about taking medication, bringing awareness and normalizing it to help remove the stigma. Kirsten Bell admitted[7] to taking a prescription for anxiety. Amanda Seyfried has said that Lexapro[8] has kept her panic attacks more manageable for over ten years. I don't believe I should first have Kristen-Bell-levels of global validation before I permit myself to accept my own needs.

All three of us need medication. Not because we want to feel special or are seeking attention or whatever else you've heard people say about mental illness, but because chemicals can run amok in our minds without consulting with you about your social standing first.

I have tried, but without medication, those chemicals get to control me. I have come off of prescriptions more times than I am willing to admit, just because I wanted to believe that my depression had gone away. To distance myself from the guilt of needing something in order to function properly. Every time, after a few months, the suicidal thoughts would return. Battling those without proper armor did not make me stronger, it made me stupid, preoccupied and vulnerable to dying prematurely.

It happened again and again, over the course of eight years. Eventually, I could no longer claim that the antidepressants I took must have only worked due to the

---

[7] *https://www.washingtonpost.com/news/arts-and-entertainment/wp/2016/05/08/kristen-bell-chris-evans-and-what-happens-when-celebrities-talk-about-anxiety-and-depression/*
[8] *https://www.today.com/health/amanda-seyfried-kept-taking-antidepressants-during-pregnancy-t114143*

placebo effect.[9] Each time I would restart medication, and after a month or so, the same people who told me to avoid pills would be first in line to tell me how happy they were to see me act like my old self again. I wanted to scream back "well they part of what makes this package, dumba**!" But that would do no good, because the only person who truly ever needed to be convinced, was me. And I have no doubt that, yep, it's absolutely F***ing real.

Next time a doctor you trust advises that it might be time to try medication, maybe listen to yourself and not the judgment that is out there. Social acceptance might be a bit behind, but it's time to take *letting things get to their absolute worst before we do something* out as a self-care option. Maybe try a different sentiment, a smarter one hopefully, no matter how self-indulgent validating your own needs seems to others.

---

[9] *https://www.webmd.com/pain-management/what-is-the-placebo-effect#1*

How My Anxiety & Depression Pushed Me To Grab The Megaphone

I'VE BEEN SUFFERING FROM depression and other mental illnesses for as long as I can remember. I wasn't truly diagnosed until I was nineteen and in college (where I could get free counseling). But I knew I wasn't feeling my best for a while.

I recall being about five and bursting into tears seemingly out of nowhere and then asking my sister "do you love me? Am I so bad that mom doesn't love me?" While this isn't exactly straight out of a DSM-V, I would say something was definitely up. As I got older and entered the "real world," it became a struggle to do anything without either beating myself up or overthinking. Eventually, I would just start dreading every simple thing. I would think about the possibility of freezing up and completely lose any ounce of motivation I had. And around in a circle I went.

Eventually, I went from wondering what I could do to feel better, to asking myself, "If I am always going to feel this, how can I make the best of it?"

Seven years into therapy, a bachelor's degree, two jobs and many promotions later, I found myself still unhappy with life. While I was taking medication to take away the physical angst, I knew that wasn't a 'fix,' just another tool to help with awful symptoms. It can't turn those off, just merely keep them quiet enough so that I could start the journey of learning who was this person, living alongside these long-term diagnoses.

In another year, my mental state was completely unraveling. I started having panic attacks at work. At first, they were concealable enough. Go to the bathroom, hyperventilate, cry. Rinse and repeat once a day. Then, one happened publicly and intensely. Suddenly it didn't matter how competent I was at my job, or whether I loved my co-workers... I simply could not go on like that.

I was finally able to take some time for myself, thanks to a yoga festival I had been planning to attend for six months. I had to plan that far in advance to get four days relief from my non-stop schedule, working 40–80 hours a week. I drove up to Vermont with a friend, and after those four hours I would be basically alone, meditating, flowing, buying mala beads, and eating incredible vegan food (that I normally did not enjoy). On day two, once my muscles were sore and I hit a wall physically, I had nowhere to run to but confront my mental state.

The festival included all the usual vinyasa, swimming and hiking activities that help us get away from the world, but it also had guest speakers. So, I ended up signing up for a class titled "Pursue Your Dreams," or something similar that I am sure I found cheesy at the time. The speaker pointed out the most obvious things: that we all deserve love, we deserve to follow our calling, leaving a lasting legacy of affecting others with the joy we have found from doing what we loved.

It made me reflect upon how truly miserable I was and how the reason for that was deeper than my depression or anxiety. It was feeling I didn't *deserve* to help others. It felt as if I lacked permission from myself to speak up about the pain and suffering I had experienced, stressed that what little family I had in my life would turn away if they learned about my condition. I couldn't even admit to myself I was sick because I wanted so badly to be accepted and not feel broken and alone, my mental illnesses fueling those thoughts even more so.

I cried a lot. And then I smiled. Because I realized that by letting myself be who I am, I could show others they are also not alone. By moving the research about various mental illnesses I was doing anyway in private into the public eye, I could help others learn that they are not "less than" or broken. Maybe, I could even convince those who found mental illness silly, that is was real and the people suffering are not simply "attention seeking," but have real medical needs.

I came home and continued fostering the idea. That fateful panic attack just sealed my direction away from marketing and towards helping others. I was finally ready to be part of the force which helps change the way things are now.

I decided that my goal was to ensure that no one should ever let themselves get to the state I was in because they were scared and alone or didn't know where to turn for care. With information and discussions, I would bridge the gap between professionals and those looking to learn more about mental illness.

The quilt came together. One square of personal experience, one of compassion sewn to online anonymity, a pocket of encouraging friends with similar backgrounds, stitched together with reliable information and apparently what you end up with is a writer and researcher who live-streams[10] a mental health (and more) talk show.

A show dedicated to exemplifying exactly how little having a mental illness changes the fact that we are all human in the end, looking for love and acceptance and are so tired of facing stigma and misinformation instead.

This took off pretty quickly, with audiences doubling the first month I was on, and my website seeing 40 percent of increased traffic month-to-month in the past four months alone. I guessed I was onto something that others in the Mental Health Community were missing as well. With the

---

[10] *Twitch.tv/mxiety. Mixer.com/Mxiety. Twitter.com/mxiety*

live stream came new, incredible connections with so many loving and engaging people that I have lost count.

I set out to help change people's understanding of their minds, but ended up feeling fulfilled through a purpose I never expected to gain in the moments when I was at my lowest.

My streams give me a permission to create, to remain resilient to all my mental illness acronyms. My inspiration is each and every person who has opened up to me, shared an opinion or brought facts as well as opinions to help perpetuate quality discussions. Together, we can help end the stigma for good.

Things You Do After Growing Up With Narcissistic Parents

NARCISSISTIC PERSONALITY DISORDER[11] is a mental health issue which does not have to be synonymous with being mean or vindictive or even a bad parent. But when all those qualities align we, as children, are forced to learn bad habits in order to survive our toxic environment.

But, make no mistake, it doesn't mean we are victims. It just means we'll need a bit of time and patience to learn how to reconcile those incorrect lessons and attain a healthier mindset.

To start, here's a list that may help identify negative coping behaviors we may have picked up through our shared experiences as children of narcissists. From this, I hope you can assess your personal well-being and start taking the necessary steps to move forward, hopefully with a trained professional.

You Think Everything Is Your Fault

Because narcissists are not capable of admitting their faults, they end up blaming others around them for their mistakes. As a child, relying on my parents to explain right from wrong, I quickly learned to accept that whatever I did was *always* wrong.

When my mother didn't get sole custody of me, it was because I didn't mention during my deposition that my father used to beat me. I was six. I didn't like to lie so I cried when we left the lawyer's office because I knew I had let her

---

[11] *https://www.mayoclinic.org/diseases-conditions/narcissistic-personality-disorder/symptoms-causes/syc-20366662*

down. I have zero recollection that my father ever laid a hand on me to this day. I am certain he never did.

So it went on. Did mother miss the deadline to submit important paperwork? It was because I didn't sit down to write it with her. Did my dad skip a ski trip? That was because he had to spend money on stupid braces for my crooked teeth.

As an adult, I must remind myself that I am not a failure before I start a task. And that doing things for people isn't the only way to earn their love. Since I never knew an adult who would own up to their own mistakes, I often even take on the responsibility for mistakes I didn't make, just in case, so that I can fix things before people around me get upset. Which leads me to…

You Feel like Everyone's Happiness Is Your Responsibility
Narcissists live in a heliocentric model of the world, with them being in the sun.

As a result, whether it was appropriate or not, my parents would push their problems onto me, asking for advice or to cheer them up by reminding them how wonderful they were. Basically, I ended up parenting my parents quite often.

I would find myself actively trying to make my mother smile even after she had demeaned me. She would complain that I was trying too hard by wearing makeup. And then follow up by asking me to do her makeup and hair to make her feel pretty.

For my father, it was letting him know that he was always doing a good job. He used to ask me to sit with him while he drank, to complain about his current marriage. Sparing no details, no matter how inappropriate they were. If I even mentioned that he might be happier away from his wife, he would remind me that being happy has nothing to do with a marriage: "You have to stick around if for no other reason, to avoid paying alimony." Naturally, after a while I agreed, and these sessions became a designated time for me to remind my father how costly a third divorce might be.

As an adult, I often have to remind myself that I cannot be expected to keep everyone happy all the time. The harder lesson was figuring out that being upset or unhappy is okay. We go through a spectrum of emotions throughout our lives and cannot possibly be expected to hold onto joy no matter the circumstances.

If You're Happy, It Is At The Expense Of Other People's Joy
Narcissists cannot consider the desires of others and will manipulate those around them to ensure that their needs always come first. I internalized this to mean that if I ever did something I might enjoy, it would hurt my parents because I did not prioritize their needs. Whenever I was happy, my emotions would quickly swing to guilt. Being happy was tied to the notion that I had inevitably let someone down.

This spell was broken when I was on a date one Thursday evening and received a call from my stepmom. She was upset I had not done my chores (specifically, clean two of the three bathrooms in the house), even though normally they were expected to be completed on Friday evenings or Saturday mornings.

She knew how much I liked my date. At home, for the past week, I could not stop talking about him and his lovely family. That call ended up being the best argument I ever had. As my stepmom started to complain about how I had yet to clean and therefore should have been home and not on *some date*, I finally felt free. It clicked that if I was ever happy, it would upset her, and there was nothing I could do to change that. Her reaction was so illogical that it clicked somehow and finally released me from continuing to attempt the unachievable.

As an adult, I am still working to un-learn this. I often self-sabotage and always look for the worst in any situation so as to prepare for the impending pain before it hits me. Basically, if I am always upset, no hurt can surprise me.

You've Self-Diagnosed Yourself with Narcissism

Self-diagnosing is easy when you have the internet. Google can do a pretty good job convincing you that you have just about anything.

Psychology research has fascinated me since high school. But, whenever I find something relating to Narcissism, I find I am holding my breath, stressed over the criteria. Checking them against my own desires. *Are these things I wish I did? Is this something inside of me that's dormant waiting to come out?*

Since I can remember, my mother loved to remind me that I was ungrateful and was being narcissistic, just like my dad. In any argument we had, she would add that I never cared about her and only loved myself, and only worried about my own needs.

I kept in touch over the phone after I moved away from Russia to the U.S. About once a month during a call she is sure to remind me how selfless she was for letting me go; for forcing herself to live alone, so that I could be happy.

I've developed an internal reprimanding voice, that reminds me of my past discretions whenever I try to put them behind me. The sad part is, I am still a bit scared for it to completely get away from it. For me, it feels like if I stop hearing the voice, I will be without a check to keep me thinking of others.

In my present therapy sessions, I work hard to combat that negative voice. I don't always win, but I am determined to quiet it down once and for all one day.

The Discussions We Should Be Having About Weight Loss

IT RECENTLY HAPPENED that I lost over **20 lbs. (~9 kg) in six months** due to an unexpected side effect from a medication I was taking. As I was adjusting to seeing my new form in the mirror, one thing I never expected was that the women I talked to about this would immediately respond to my concern with things like: "You look so great, didn't you want to lose weight?" or "that's amazing!" or "if you keep complaining, I can give you some of mine," and finally, "I'm so jealous!"

I wasn't talking about it to brag, I didn't know how I felt about the weight being gone and wanted perspective, which is exactly what I got.

These women were not strangers either. They were people I care deeply about, whose opinions matter to me. I don't believe they previously judged my weight one way or another. But, at the same time as I was nervously going to doctors and getting blood tests to make sure I was okay, they were asking about "my methods" and "secret". I would try to play it off with humor, explaining that all they had to do was make all your food taste like ash, as it had for me recently. I freaked out a bit when the response to this, several times, was: "but at least you look good."

It was as though they did not care that this weight loss was unhealthy, or that something out of my control was causing it. The cost always justified the results.

With dieting culture so ingrained into our minds as part of the standard of being a woman, I am not sure what other response I could have possibly expected. I did know that this was not the reaction I would have offered a friend in my situation.

No, of course, I am not looking for sympathy and condolences as I describe this. I understand how, I even sound rather whiny for even having this complaint. I get it. And yet…

That's Exactly What Worries Me.
Medically speaking[12], a healthy weight-loss strategy would involve losing around 1 to 2 lbs. (>1 kg.) a week. Using the BMI scale[13], doctors can determine when such weight loss is medically necessary. In my scenario, my previous BMI was very much in the healthy rage (23 points). Thankfully, my current weight is still in the same range (19 points), but it's quickly inching closer to "underweight" rather than "normal."

The New York Times[14] reported back in 2013 how just thinking about food, the way diets force you to do, uses precious mental bandwidth that could be better spent thinking about…well, literally anything else. Since women are more likely to go on diets, I think we know whose work is more likely suffering from this constant calorie obsession and hunger.

So, If I Am Still Healthy and Everyone Wants to Lose Weight, Why Was I Taken Aback by People's Responses?
That answer is two-fold. First, I was actually a bit confused as to how I should feel about it myself, which is likely also why I was oversharing in the first place. Second, I feel like this brought to light a much larger issue. If a woman loses weight in our society, it's tertiary, no, probably quinary, to ask them if they are otherwise feeling well. Again, I am not blaming

---

[12] *https://www.cdc.gov/healthyweight/losing_weight/index.html*
[13] *https://www.cdc.gov/obesity/downloads/bmiforpactitioners.pdf*
[14] *https://www.nytimes.com/2013/09/22/business/the-mental-strain-of-making-do-with-less.html?pagewanted=all&_r=0*

any one woman for how they expressed their excitement over my finally achieving this standard goal, I am blaming a flawed society that has pressed us to obsessively validate our bodies against one another.

I had struggled with actual eating disorders and found that no one at the time, in high school, or within the family I lived with then, felt that they were problematic either. They were the means to an end. Just think about how many women and men suffer from eating disorders[15]. Now, I didn't have an eating disorder this time around, but clearly, my weight loss should have seemed too oddly rapid to be enviable?

I remember being fourteen, underweight and malnourished having just moved to the U.S., and already feeling confused about my relationship with food. I was told I needed to eat because I was too skinny, only to be reminded that no one would ever love me if I gained too much weight.

Throughout the rest of my teens, as life in my parent's house continued filling up with emotional abuse, I took my stress out on my own body through a combination of purging, starving, and over-exercising. I no longer had an eating disorder after I graduated college, but I found new ways to push my body. I spent a year training for a 10K, attending two separate gyms, three days a week to take barre, Pilates, and yoga classes to get in shape for my wedding.

The Turn
I finally realized just last year that all of these activities, while some healthier than others, had done virtually nothing to adjust the number on my scale. That perhaps the number was not as important as how I felt and how I treated my body. I chose to take care of myself with a healthy amount of exercise

---

[15] *https://anad.org/education-and-awareness/about-eating-disorders/eating-disorders-statistics/*

and better eating habits. It seemed I had finally come to terms with my shape and size even though I felt it was against the ideals I had once held for so long. And it was absolutely in part thanks to having better role models[16] (and media representation[17]).

As I looked in the mirror after losing the first 10 lbs. from my already rather small frame, I felt disgusted. I could see each of my ribs and fully pinch my collarbone. Where did my butt go? I had just started liking it. And why, now that I looked the way I thought I always wanted to, was I not happy?

What would sixteen-year-old Marie say to herself right now? I once thought she would be envious and consider this an achievement, but instead, I now think she would be sad. After earning a healthier body image, this felt like some kind of delayed, weight karma.

Yes, I know you are sick and tired of hearing women blame the media and society for pressuring us to lose weight constantly. But are we also tired of empathizing with each other? How did it happen that looking thin became more important than our health?

What we women have done to make it worse, is disseminate the unrealistic standards by pressuring each other to conform to them. Dieting and under-eating are considered to be the necessary default, not just an option. Women are taught that having conversations about our bodies, what we eat, and how we maintain weight is polite small talk. Needing to want big lips, tiny noses, giant eyes, while being curvy but with no waist is a standard expectation.

---

[16] *https://www.vanityfair.com/hollywood/2018/02/jennifer-lawrence-cover-story*
[17] *https://www.ae.com/aerie-real-life/*

I was in a Trader Joe's when I woman standing at the sample counter asked a patron how she kept so thin. Granted, I did not hear the starting point of their conversation, but the woman shopping did not hesitate to explain that she is actually self-conscious because she gained a few pounds over the holidays and "can't seem to shake them off." That made the saleswoman put her hand on the shopper's shoulder and quietly nod in solidarity before rattling off how the radish dish she was offering to sample had become a staple for everyone in her family. She gained a customer through an exchange that would have been more appropriate if they were both talking about losing pets. Why couldn't the saleswoman respond by saying something like "but you look healthy" or "as long as you feel fine." Why did she default to eulogizing her customer's feelings of loss?

Considering how much time we spend thinking about food and discussing our bodies, maybe both men and women should be shifting the conversation to focus overall on health, mental and physical.

The message we currently perpetuate among ourselves literally sucks: suck in your feelings and suck in your gut. We need some adjustment to focus less on appearances and more on internal wealth. We need to change our standard from admiring people for pushing their minds and bodies too far, to focus more on encouraging each other to be healthy, whatever that means for the individual you're speaking with.

Let's take both our minds and bodies back and not let them be held hostage by diet culture. Next time you see someone who seems thin, and has lost a lot of weight rapidly, catch that idea of wanting to ask what their secret is. Stop yourself as you notice your thoughts focusing on your girlfriend's body altogether, and instead, really mean it when you ask them: "How are you doing?"

How My Eating Disorder Started and Where It Ended

EXPOSURE TO MEDIA IS NOT what convinced me I wasn't pretty enough.

I never looked at the pictures in magazines to compare myself to the women I saw. I was really only interested in the shiny watches the models were wearing, or if I there were any perfume-samples I could rub on my wrist. Looking back, I can safely say that the insecurities I had about my body by the time I was fourteen started developing thanks to aunts, cousins, uncles, and my mother.

Actually, I don't really blame anyone. I am not seeking some teleological answer for the body issues I experienced. Statistically speaking, it's not uncommon for children with emotional turmoil to develop mental health issues[18] in adulthood. And then there are the statistics for young women developing eating disorders[19]. With the luck of the genetic draw and my early life experiences in Russia, I must embrace being part of these statistics.

The true culprit?

Illogical lessons taught at an early age, which eventually created unhealthy thought patterns. To grow up in a big Greek family is to be known and discussed by every one of those family members. *Are you eating too much? Too little? Why do you only play with boys? Why can't you get along with the girls? Eh, you should get your hands dirty in the mud while you're so young! Oh, my goodness, you are filthy! How could you give your mother this much laundry to do?* With so many opinions to

---

[18] *https://www.psychologytoday.com/us/blog/when-food-is-family/201303/ptsd-and-eating-disorders*
[19] *https://www.nimh.nih.gov/health/statistics/eating-disorders.shtml*

listen to, and none properly filtered by my mother or father, I started to feel like I could never do the right thing. Initially, I was a bookworm and only cared about my body enough to ensure it was in working condition to climb trees, carry around dirt, and ride on tire swings.

My first encounter with the concept of an eating disorder was while I was reading an unofficial Spice Girls biography and learning that Geri Halliwell used bulimia as a way to keep weight off when she was a young model. Being eight at the time, I had no idea what that word meant, but I was perplexed by the description. I was taking in new information and just re-reading it over and over to make sense of it. And I couldn't. The only time I ever threw up was when I was sick, and that felt horrible, so why would anyone choose to do that?

By the time I turned nine, the message that my body was meant to be worthy of admiration became pervasive. Someone in my family would make a comment about my "growing womanly hips," or my future ability to give birth to "nice, healthy Greek boys." Every time, I was completely taken aback: Why were my changing body parts so important to others? *I don't think I have control over this. Please stop talking about them.*

I had an uncle who would smack my butt whenever I would walk by. I responded with a puzzled look, he'd add "to help it grow nice and big!" Another uncle, when asked how my hair looked after I dyed it, said "it's nice, but you have to get rid of that tummy if you really want to make a change."

Meanwhile, my mother was also sure to remind me how I wouldn't be able to eat like this forever" whenever I ate pasta in the evening. It's not like I had access to decadent food either. My mother didn't cook and wasn't great about shopping for healthy options.

At this point, I was between twelve and thirteen. I weighed less than 100 lbs at 5 ft tall (43.4 kg, 153 cm).

Culturally this was normal. In Russia and within my Greek family, girls were raised in a manner which made them attractive to boys. You would fail as a parent if your girl was not obedient and didn't look like she cared to get married. Naturally, this meant my mother would pay for belly-dancing classes even though she balked when my piano teacher had the audacity to ask to be paid.

If that doesn't seem natural, or normal to you, know I didn't find it that way either and was therefore considered a rebel. I would never say that dancing isn't wonderful, it's more a problem that my mother never asked me what I wanted, but instead focused on shaping my body as a way to obtain the approval of others.

As my hormones changed, conflicting and uncomfortable messages from adults continued, creating clashes and confusion, as well as a distortion in understanding the purpose of my body.

Somewhere in the middle of all of this, I moved countries. Away from my mother and towards a father whose family was not looking forward to getting to know me. This is what proved to be the most fertile soil to make matters worse. I wanted to be accepted and loved, and as it became clearer that wasn't going to happen, I started to take the anger and disappointment out on my body. After all, I had been consistently taught that it was the best tool to obtain love from others.

Life in my father's home was a horrible cycle. Overcompensating for the often lack of food in the USSR, many Russian families in the U.S. cook lavish dinners almost weekly. Every weekend there would be at least one large meal during which I overate, partially to compensate for years of malnourishment and partially because I would offend the cook if I didn't. And the cook got very angry when offended. She also did not shy away from offering what she thought to be great advice about food. When one evening I jokingly noted that I couldn't keep eating but wished I could, she responded with: "If you throw up, you can make room for more."

What. A. Great. Idea.
If I wanted to keep eating, but still desired to stay skinny so that someone would love me, I needed to remove that food from my body, or so I hypothesized. Purging accomplished that, sure, but so would running and doing extensive amounts of sit-ups. I had already started developing anxiety-induced asthma at the time, so exercising did not come easily, but I had my Russian tummy-hating uncle visiting often enough that I kept motivated.

On days when I would run, I would often have to stop midway through to gather myself. Still dizzy and unable to breathe, I would force myself to keep going. I knew I wouldn't pass out, and if I did, it would be easy enough to write it off as finally reaching the optimal punishment.

The following three years of my life were rather graphic, please be warned. Skip the next paragraph should you prefer to avoid details. I promise to be less graphic right after.

By fifteen I was caught in a cycle: Fight with my Stepmom, Eat, Cry while vomiting. I remember the feeling of stomach acid as it hit the back of my teeth, falling yellow and clear into the bowl. I was never satisfied until every last morsel of food I had consumed was out of my body. I clung with brittle nails to the toilet bowl I was tasked to clean weekly but never could "correctly". Sweat kept my thinning hair clinging to my face. Crying and vomiting while the sink ran so that no one could hear. Only when I felt like I had punished myself enough for not being good enough would I stop.

I want every little girl to know how horrible binging and purging truly feels. There is a burning sensation as the bile rises up to your mouth and nose. You have to look as your food comes out half-digested and you don't stop until nothing but yellow bile is left. Which is what corrodes your teeth. The taste of your insides doesn't leave your mouth for a while. Not even after you've eaten. It can last for days. There is nothing sexy or glorious about emptying the contents of your stomach. Our bodies are not built to do it and fight every step of the way to try to get us to stop. Unfortunately, it takes the mind some time to catch up with the body.

As an adult, I often imagine thousands of young girls repeating this act while living in abusive households. None of us ever received the approval we craved, even after we performed our penance. None of us had mothers who could check on us and worry, hold our hair, then help us wash up and let us know that such sacrifices were unnecessary for anyone to truly love you. All of us not yet wise enough to start learning to love ourselves.

I was one of those women and I was alone. I was also vehemently convinced that what I was doing was entirely normal and benign. And if I ever doubted it, I would re-convince myself that this is how every woman spends her time in the bathroom, and that made it completely ordinary.

Sitting on tile, clutching my stomach in immense pain as my body rebelled. The only true and consistent consequences of my actions were unrelated to weight-loss. I never lost a pound. I never felt better. Instead, I had cavities in my teeth, coarse hair, peeling nails, and painful acid reflux, which to this day remains as a reminder of my mistakes.

I am so grateful my body fought a good fight. Lots of internal scarring, sure, but it was working against a broken mind, trying to keep me alive, no matter how stupid my actions were.

Most of my family except for my sister knew and lauded my actions. Running was an approved sport substitute. On the other hand, crying a lot and then going to the bathroom was just being overdramatic. Throwing up did not appear to be connected to either of those activities, which is why everything never came together as an issue.

It Ended Rather Abruptly
I was seventeen and had finished my third course of prescription antacids in a year when my sister sat me down to talk. She never used the word bulimic, she just told her story and caught me with a throwaway phrase: "and I am pissed you keep wasting the food I buy us."

At the time I was living with my sister and visiting my parents on the weekend. At one point our parents promised they would help us with rent, but they periodically forgot to. The two of us were living on her $35,000 a year salary with a monthly $1,100 rent payment for a one bedroom just because it was in a good school district and our parents promised to help. Needless to say, we didn't have a lot of money for food, and the realization that I was literally flushing our careful purchases down the drain filled me with guilt.

Now, bulimia doesn't come with an OFF switch, but that realization was finally enough for me to want to stop. I went to teachers I thought would understand and connected with a few girls I thought I could trust and started to talk about it. I got better, but I didn't fully stop the habit until I was midway through college.

The total body damage was the following:

- It took about a year my last purge for my nails to grow in normal.
- Two years for me to grow out hair that wasn't brittle and split at the ends.
- A year for fluoride toothpaste to help my teeth, which had been damaged by stomach acid.

And that was just the damage I could heal from. As I mentioned, I still have the acid reflux and have not been able to digest lactose since. Rounding the whole thing out is, what else, Irritable Bowel Syndrome.

I have often referred to myself as broken. Sometimes in a derogatory way, other times with hope and implication that I can be fixed. My mental health never had a solid foundation, but I now own the fact that I was the one who broke my body.

The whole optimism of "but I learned this lesson" only applies if there was a reason to try and make the mistake. I don't feel like this particular thing had to happen in my life to teach me a lesson. It happened because I misused my body as an outlet for my anger and hoping to find adoration.

I don't regret a lot of things that have happened to me, and I certainly have forgiven myself for doing this, but I really wish I never started the cycle. The cultural permeation of what I needed to be is what created the idea that I would need to "fix" my body at one point, but it was the constant reinforcement of this belief that drove me to act.

Since it is customary for these entries to have happy endings, I can note one positive outcome.

Had this not happened to me, I would not be able to write about it. Without writing about it, I couldn't spread awareness about what bulimia is truly like and perhaps deter someone from deciding to pursue it.

Consider how you speak to the women and men in your life. Do you let them know they are okay the way they are, no matter what ideal they are feeling pressured to conform to? Or when someone looks thinner, do you compliment them before even asking how they feel? These are all pieces of daily life that had a hand in reinforcing my actions. My need to punish my body was born from the idea that my body was never right.

Think about what you wish someone would have said to you as a child and offer insight to someone you know now. You don't have to be bossy, but you can start a positive discussion around this difficult topic. **Make a better default.**

The Importance of Combating PTSD Socially

ONE MORNING, I WENT OUT for pancakes and ended up sharing a booth wall with an energetic gentleman and his family. While waiting for my food to arrive, I couldn't help but listen in on his table. He had lots of opinions and was telling stories when one of his family members asked: "So, what happened at work?"

The conversation died. After a full minute, he finally responded. "Jerry, threw me under the bus with the whole PTSD thing."

Silence.

"He really messed up the car I was working on and I was getting so pissed, and he was all up in my face saying, 'What? You going to have an episode?!' Sure, I know I get heated and it's hard to control that, but I he didn't have to throw it in my face like that."

A younger man at the table put his hand on his shoulder "you know that guy's a jerk, don't let him get to you."

"I know. It's just not fair, because I know they took his side," was the last thing I heard on the matter.

The truth about Post Traumatic Stress Disorder (PTSD)[20] is that anyone can experience it. Even the United States Department of Veteran Affairs has chosen to simply post the definition directly from the DSM-V[21] without any sort of asterisk or simplification for those not serving in the military. No one is shielded and even indirect trauma (such as simply hearing about a loved one being hurt) can cause its onset.

---

[20] *https://www.psychiatry.org/patients-families/ptsd/what-is-ptsd*
[21] *https://www.ptsd.va.gov/index.asp*

However, the link between military service and PTSD occurrence cannot be ignored, considering the 65 percent suicide rate in veterans over the age of 50 (from a 2014 study[22]).

Only recently[23] has more money been allotted to help with staffing issues and establish hotlines. Animal researchers[24], psychologists and the aforementioned department are fighting to enforce more preventative measures to help end the epidemic. Of course, it's still not enough. Veteran's Affairs estimates that of those who have seen combat, about 11–20 percent will experience PTSD symptoms in a year. Soldiers often remain quiet to avoid scaring their family, or as appearing weak, as emotions are often associated with lack of strength in our culture[25]. Those who do seek help likely do so only if they can be certain about their anonymity. Given this stigma and lack of resources for those fighting to protect our freedoms, how can a regular civilian, as for help in good conscience? Thing is, PTSD doesn't care whether you are a soldier or a survivor of another tragedy — the symptoms are horrible.

I thought asking for help would wrongly divert attention. Instead, I attempted to just pretend it wasn't a problem for me. I was spontaneously bursting into tears, losing track of my thoughts mid-sentence, and waking up in a cold sweat after reliving my worst fears in my dreams. Sure,

---

[22] *https://www.va.gov/opa/pressrel/pressrelease.cfm?id=2951*

[23] *https://journals.lww.com/ajnonline/Fulltext/2016/10000/Analysis_Finds_About_20_Veterans_Died_Daily_from.12.aspx*

[24] *https://www.sciencedirect.com/science/article/abs/pii/S1555415515009599*

[25] *https://www.forbes.com/home_usa/?toURL=https://www.forbes.com/sites/kareanderson/2012/09/28/five-reasons-why-stoicism-matters-today/&refURL=https://www.google.com/&referrer=https://www.google.com/#d63e779324be*

I had read about how children with traumatic pasts[26] are likely to have PTSD later in their lives, but I just couldn't believe that applied to me. I kept thinking that people with that diagnosis were usually resilient, brave, and most likely had gone through war. They were not small, blonde, white girls who sit on the floor rocking back and forth, crying until their eyes are dry. They would have been through worse and handled it better.

No part of me wanted to recognize that perhaps I would feel stronger and more in control if I chose to confront the fear. And was absolutely against acknowledging the possibility that my childhood was atypical, for that would create a domino effect and force me to re-evaluate all of the emotional lessons I learned up to that point.

I would have to learn how people should speak to each other, and how to celebrate a holiday in a way that didn't involve drinking too much, and how parents could manage anger without throwing their children against a wall. And I was not ready to confront any of those memories more than I already had to inside flashbacks.

Accepting the issue would also require me to accept the social judgment and stigma that goes with mental illness, and I was holding on by a thread trying to fit in as it was.

Any time I dipped my toe to test the waters of social sympathy, someone would remind me to never speak ill of my parents. Or that I would see it differently once I had kids of my own. My favorite would take my sharing with them as a time to measure up against me. As though we were competing for the title of "most miserable". There were some who just dismissed me as someone clearly lacking proper self-judgment. If none of that sounds appealing to you (and I should hope it doesn't), then you might understand why I

---

[26] *https://www.semanticscholar.org/paper/Child-abuse-and-neglect-and-the-brain--a-review.-Glaser/cdd703ea329a170dae0f946693145a070e1d3556*

chose instead to push aside my feelings and only let them out at home, where no one could see, after spending the day cracking my teeth smiling.

The National PTSD Foundation estimates that as much as 7.8 percent of Americans will experience PTSD at some point in their lives.[27] The current data also shows that women suffer at double the rate of men.

But data alone is not going to help me convince my roommate I am not dangerous when I am experiencing a flashback, just as it will not convince a soldier to go talk to someone when they have nightmares after returning home. Like most mental illnesses, we don't talk about PTSD in a productive, non-derogatory way outside of the mental health support social media community.

A huge reason flashbacks are so painful[28] is that they are reminders of how helpless you felt as the trauma happened, and how little control you have when it reappears. It's hard to distinguish reality from a memory. It makes you question the accuracy of other memories you have stored.

Thanks to therapy and mindfulness I learned ways to help me return to the present moment faster. This type of therapy meant that, yes, I would have to willingly go back and re-live some of the worst moments of my life. Once I had fully moved through the moment and learned which emotions were forcing my mind to relive it over and over again, I could move on. I learned how to recognize a flashback compared to reality, I learned what triggered it, and I learned why I couldn't let it go.

This actually put **me more in control than pretending nothing was going on**. I got to decide when I would go into a 30–45 min session, making it happen on *my* terms. When you pretend it's not real, you're vulnerable to having the

---

[27] *https://www.ptsd.va.gov/*
[28] *https://mxiety.com/blog/what-a-flashback-feels-like*

thoughts you so dutifully shoved away resurface at the drop of any remotely related trigger.

Only recently, after more than three years, did I truly regain this control, finally letting go of certain memories in my life. It's not that I never have episodes, but they're much less frequent and I am better prepared for them — **they're happening on my terms.**

My call is for anyone who is suffering to come forward and start a discussion. I believe it will be much easier for more veterans — more people — to seek care if they see other men and women doing so with confidence. Like with everything else, setting an example of self-care is a great place to start.

What I Learned About Forgiveness Through My Abusive Parents

I HAD THE LUCK OF not one, not two, but three abusive parents to handle growing up. Rest assured, all three had a brand of awfulness that was truly their own, but they also had many qualities in common: deflection, minimizing my problems or needs and letting everyone know how much of a martyr they were for raising such an ungrateful daughter. In the past three years I have cut off contact completely with one of them, seen another about twice a year, and call the other about once a month.

There is another book waiting to be written with many more specific stories but wanted to share some to start. There is research confirming that encountering traumatic environments in which the child cannot speak up due to fear is detrimental to that child's mental health[29]. Little research has been done to discern the difference between non-traditional families because there are so many types (mine being the step-kind) but imagine that threat at three times the force.

As a child, you are usually unaware of the notion that your parents might *not* know what's best. Usually, we are much older when we find that they are fallible people, like everyone else. But my parents weren't just imperfect. They induced isolation and pain into my life. Pain which planted seeds of distrust.

The first time I understood that something wasn't right I was about eight. It was the moment when my mother flew with me to Russia and then left me with family I didn't

---

[29] *https://www.sciencedirect.com/science/article/abs/pii/S0277953605002534*

know without saying goodbye. I was told that it was the stress and exhaustion that made her act so rashly, but even then I didn't buy it. By her own logic, if our dad loved us, he wouldn't have left the family. If she left, didn't that mean she didn't love the family? Or was it specifically just me?

I learned a clearer truth about my father when seven years later I was reintroduced to him. He came to help move me back to the U.S. He explained himself to be the victim in my kidnapping, as he didn't know until child services called his home to ask where I was. He seemed kind, and he gave me hugs I never received from my mother. Then I moved in with him. I recall him being upset when my stepmother and I would argue. He would drive me back to my sister's apartment, talking about how unhappy he was in his life, only to call me two days later and told me that sometimes people get upset, and we just needed to forgive them for that and move on. Yes, even if knives were thrown in our direction.

There were other constant reminders that I had my place and needed to remember exactly where it was. For example, an odd sibling rivalry which was cultivated by the adults around both us. When I needed a laptop for school, my younger half-sister then received a computer twice the cost the next day. When I asked to take a college-level course, I was told I couldn't because my sister needed to go to summer camp. I was the one responsible to clean the toilets as part of our chores. To this day, I am in tens of thousands of dollars of debt from college, while my younger sibling is having her entire undergraduate degree paid for, as well as her master's degree.

Yet still, I was living in this situation and didn't think anything of it. I just assumed I was not working hard enough.

And how confusing were those emotions when I would hear how important I was to the family, only to be screamed at when I got upset that someone had clearly used my toothbrush. How odd is it that if said how someone made fun of me at school, I would be told that I was too nerdy for anyone to like anyway. That it was important that I married someone who would take care of me, but when I was crying because my first boyfriend broke up with me, I was told that it was because I should have known to "put out if I wanted to keep him."

The event that finally pushed me away came when I bought my first car at twenty-three. My stepmother was upset I bought the car when she had specifically told me I don't need one. So, she didn't even come close to look at it. Two days later, I received a call to loan the car to my sibling. I politely said "No" – a word I didn't know was in my vocabulary at the time. Before she could finish screaming into the phone about how ungrateful I was, I had asked her to never speak to me again.

Whether my situation seems unlikely, odd or not a big deal to you, know that the real decision to cut/reduce communication comes not when you're mistreated. Not when the mistakes are made. Not when we realize our parents are also fallible human beings. They come once those planted seeds become full grown. Seeds of doubt, mistrust, and pain make for rotten, twisted, thorned trees once we've reached adulthood.

It's the moment when, as a twenty-three-year-old woman, with my own home, a stable, bill-paying job and years of therapy obtained, I approached those I loved about my pain. I showed them the tree and offered to chop it down and plant and care for another one together.

The relationship was lost at the same time I realized that I had forgiven them. Because I knew what I would hear next and did not fault them for it. The fault was mine for going to someone broken, asking to be made whole.

Each in their own unique way, and yet, saying the same things, they explained that I was the cause of all of my own suffering[30]. It was because I only wanted to see the bad in them. I was selfish and always needed their attention and they couldn't keep up with my demands. They told me about all the awful things I did as a child to earn this treatment. I once called one of them a "pig" and told another that they should have thought about not being able to clothe me before they had me. I was just too bossy and always wanted things my way. I agreed to disagree.

What they didn't know, is that I had already planted wonderful, bountiful trees with others. Orchards indeed. Other than these three (or so) people, no one who truly loved me, blood-related or not, had ever expressed that I needed to change my ways on account of just being too stupid to speak with, or too selfish or "too" anything else. People who loved me just loved me.

I also went to apologize to others I had hurt along the way, to seek a way to mend relationships I knew I was responsible for breaking. I worked on taking my own advice. Taking the ax and chopping down those thorny trees to plant new ones. With my parents, I learned to establish boundaries. The harder part is holding myself to them since someone who does not care for your feelings will not care to respect a boundary you have set.

Disconnecting from a person who happens to be a parent is not a common topic for discussion, indeed, it is rather taboo. I have found in this instance there are rather dramatic camps of opinions. The first says if you have a toxic parent, you should cut them from your life with no shame. The other camp is positive that forgiveness is the only way to

---

[30] *https://www.thehotline.org/2014/05/29/what-is-gaslighting/*

go, and that it's possible to change others through kindness. The idea that you can change someone whom you wish to have loved you the way you love them has a strong pull, I get it.

You may not yet believe your needs are important enough because the most important people never advised you were, but I am here to tell you, you are. You don't need to believe me either, I just know it.

A Disney Princess Inspired Me to Leave My Abusive Family

WHEN WE WERE LITTLE, many of us picked a Disney Princess to identify with. In the past few years, Mickey has been doing a great job diversifying his lineup, ensuring that more kids find their inner strength through incredible female role models. Growing up I could see myself as Cinderella, cleaning and waiting for a prince to come and take me away from a family where I never felt quite wanted. But I grew out of Cinderella and wanting to be passively saved. And on November 24, 2010, I found my princess in the animated movie *Tangled*, and, with her, the strength I needed to stand up for myself.

Rapunzel was the role model I didn't know I needed, while, the feature's villain, Mother Gothel, was a perfect foil and a powerful catalyst.

When you live in a home with parents who are mentally but not physically abusive, it's hard to express to others what the problem might be. In my case, relatives and close family friends could even justify my parent's actions by saying that I was "just a teenager" or "just impatient". Other times, those who wanted to help truly weren't sure what they *could* do.

Mother Gothel gave a name to my misery.

Gothel kidnaps Rapunzel from her family and raises her hidden in a remote tower, using the girl's magical healing powers to keep herself forever young. Although she uses loving words and has successfully convinced Rapunzel she is her birth mother, there is no doubt that this woman only cares for Rapunzel as a vessel for her power, as she frequently holds Rapunzel's magically healing hair, kisses her on top of her head, and yet, otherwise avoids any other physical contact.

Through fear tactics, Gothel is able to keep the stolen princess from wanting to venture outside of the tower she was raised in. However, after being locked up for eighteen years, on her birthday, Rapunzel gathers all of her courage to ask Gothel to escort her to see the "floating lights" she had been following since she was little.

In comes a mercurial musical number, *Mother Knows Best*, where Gothel works to solidify herself as the victim.

Gothel, immediately goes on the defense and guilts her ward into believing that she would break her mother's heart, not to mention that the world outside could destroy her feeble sensitivities. The concern is almost believable if you forget that locking Rapunzel in this the tower has deprived the missing princess of an education, socialization and the love of her birth family.

The lyrics are simultaneously loving, yet peppered with insults to Rapunzel's body and allude to her lack of self-sufficiency, which as the parent figure, Gothel was responsible for in the first place.

"Sloppy, underdressed, immature, clumsy
Please, they'll eat you up alive
Gullible, naive, positively grubby
Ditzy and a bit, well, hmm, vague
Plus, I believe gettin' kinda chubby
I'm just saying 'cause I love you…"

I remember at that moment thinking: "That's so unkind." Followed by an epiphany as I considered how I wasn't allowed to go to a college four hours away because I "wouldn't make it there." Or how after looking at me for a minute I was once asked: "I don't know how you'll get anyone to love you if you keep gaining weight and have acne."

Gothel finishes the number by losing her temper and scolding Rapunzel for ever asking to leave — guilting[31] her into believing that the mere idea was not an acceptable one to have. All culminating with an affirmation of love for her "daughter."

A while later, Rapunzel tries to show her mother an example of how she can subdue the aforementioned scary thugs with a knocked out intruder (Flynn Rider) in their closet. Suddenly it becomes undeniable that Gothel only cares to keep the girl for herself. She concludes "You are not ever leaving this tower!" proving that her previous implication of Rapunzel's lacking self-sufficiency had nothing to do with her decision.

This message of care mixed with hurtful comments and contradictory promises is what creates the cognitive dissonance that actually pushes Rapunzel away. It's also what torments her when she does finally find the courage to leave.

Leaving the tower is not the end, however. Years of mental abuse cannot be undone in a day, even in the Disney-verse, especially if your abuser still has contact with you. Towards the climax of the movie, Gothel reaffirms her earlier warnings by reprising her musical number[32], but this time with the intention to pinpoint and manipulates Rapunzel's "fragile" emotions.

"Likes you?
Please, Rapunzel, that's demented
This is why you never should have left

---

[31] *https://alfredmacdonald.com/2012/11/07/gaslighting-what-it-isnt/*
[32] *https://genius.com/Walt-disney-records-mother-knows-best-reprise-lyrics*

Dear, this whole romance that you've invented
Just proves you're too naive to be here

Why would he like you? Come on now, really?
Look at you, you think that he's impressed?
Don't be a dummy
Come with mummy…"

Similarly, to the first number, Gothel switches between lowering Rapunzel's self-esteem, calling her a "dummy," and telling her there is no way Flynn Rider could possibly love someone like her. Gothel's tone turns worse once she hears Rapunzel say something she's never heard before:

"No."

I felt the impact of that "No" in my core.

A few months prior, I recall sitting in my car in a grocery store parking lot, waiting to see my now-husband for a date. I called home to let the family know I might be coming back late. In response, my stepmother berated me for not doing a thorough enough job cleaning the bathroom by my room and therefore not earning my leave. She demanded I come home to finish at once. It was a Friday night. I realized that *if* I had done a poor job I could easily do it again the next day.

So, I said: **"No."**

Looking back to that moment, it felt like my stepmother's response almost echoed Gothel's. She advised that I was betraying our family. She threatened abandonment as a way to remind me who held the control over my future, even though I was almost twenty-one and had been paying for my own college education along with just about every other expense.

Rapunzel proved herself independent because she was able to take on her adventure alone, but that independence was still new. Same went for me going away to college despite warnings I "wouldn't make it."

My stepmom hung up on me, telling me I didn't need to come home, **ever**. Gothel's expression caves as she sings in response. It is clear she is afraid, knowing she is about to lose eighteen years of control. All with that one simple "no."

"Trust me, my dear
That's how fast he'll leave you
I won't say I told you so

Rapunzel knows best!
So if he's such a dreamboat
Go and put him to the test
If he's lying
Don't come crying

Mother knows best…"

Rapunzel is practically forced to go through with trusting Flynn to accompany her, and yet the seed of doubt was planted in her mind through this song.

Once again, this felt all too familiar. All three of my parents found ways to undermine the relationship I was in once it was clear this person had the potential to make me happy. Even if I as I was trying to presume that they were truly looking out for me, they were literally placing bets on how long my new relationship would last. They would say that I couldn't possibly be really happy, which made me scared and doubtful of my reality at times.

Yet, I desperately wanted their approval and love. And even after that "no," I took actions, hoping to gain those things.

It's the same reason that when Mother Gothel dies, despite what she put Rapunzel through, you can still see a glint of hope in Rapunzel's eyes, a look you may have seen on someone who, while leaving an abusive relationship, still feels love for the abuser, who still hopes love will come from them.

Back in the theater, during my first viewing (of about 200 since), the parallels sunk in. By the time the credits rolled, I was resolved to change my circumstance, as Rapunzel had.

I am sure studio execs had no idea that with their 3D-animated human had just handed some Russian immigrant girl in New Jersey the tools she needed to understand that she was not treated well.

I needed proof that I wasn't actually loved, because the way my parents presented it, what else could love have been like?

And to the outside world, these were my parents, so surely they loved me unconditionally. Both assumptions were based on a projection of what society hopes family relationships should and must be like. Both were severely wrong in my case.

Rapunzel chooses to leave her tower, to follow a stranger to a world she's never known without truly knowing even why. It's clear she is not motivated to leave because she hopes to marry the thief who entered her home, or that she suspects anything wrong about her mother. She steps out because there was a force inside of her telling her there was something out there bigger than the circumstance she was in.

I feel that this is the best lesson a Disney princess could teach a little girl—sometimes you have to take the leap even though you are not sure if it will work out. You have to believe that you know what's best for you and trust your gut. It also doesn't hurt to reject those labels the world puts on us, be it a thief, thug, or vague dummy.

The Love and Life I Would Have Missed If I had Committed Suicide

OUT OF THE RECENT TEN YEARS I have spent one year following my dream, over nine with the love of my life, and four in an incredible home we built together. I still expect that this means I will eventually stop being preoccupied with suicidal ideation[33] or thoughts of ending one's life, with or without intent to actually do something, but that just isn't the case. I have pictured myself careening off the road in my car or using the butcher's knife we have in our block. Never would I act upon it, but the thoughts are disturbing nonetheless.

With medication to guide me and a therapist I see regularly, I thought that anything pertaining to such darkness would be a thing of the past. And honestly, it largely is. But once in a while, the monster rears its head. It sneaks into the corner of my mind. The space where it's dark, where there are cobwebs and old boxes that I don't dare look into anymore. In that corner is where the monster plants its decrepit body and starts digging. It will unearth whatever it is that is relevant to my current life's roadblocks and start throwing them around until there is so much chaos back in my mind that I cannot help but think about a permanent solution, feeling like death is the only way to be relieved from the torture.

To counter this, I have decided to take note of the biggest events in my life I would have missed had I given into this beast when it took total control first in 2014, and then again in 2017.

---

[33] *https://www.nimh.nih.gov/health/statistics/suicide.shtml*

My magical engagement and wedding
Back early in 2014, my then boyfriend picked me off the bathroom floor in our apartment one evening. I was quite the sight, mascara streaking, hair everywhere, blubbering. He was scared. I was scared. I scared myself because I wanted to die but called myself too much of a coward to go through with it (there is nothing cowardly about pushing past your thoughts to survive).

I mumbled something to the effect of: "I don't know why you are dealing with me."

As he carried me to the bed he responded, "I always thought you would make a great mother, but not if you are like this."

It was hurtful but sobered me right up. While wiping away snot I asked, "You would marry me?" The realization was the first time I thought of marriage having a place in my future. I just assumed people *like me* didn't deserve that kind of joy.

"Of course, but, not this person. This isn't you."

I'm not going to say those words cured me or even inspired me, because that would be stupid. But they gave me a purpose and they hit the soul of what I actually was running from. In my flashbacks, in my night terrors, I always woke up after a relative or someone close to me told me they hated me. Well, here I had the opportunity to be loved and I was letting depression take that away from me. That could not keep happening.

I promised myself two things at this point: I would get better, and I would find a way to give back the love that I had been offered to those who felt alone due to their past pain or mental illness.

I started paying better attention to my therapist. I didn't argue with my psychiatrist when he prescribed medication. I took a three-week leave from work. By the end,

WELL THAT EXPLAINS IT

with three-to-four therapy sessions a week and without skipping medication, I started to feel better.

The proposal was magical. He got the idea to do so at a lantern festival because of my favorite movie, which made me feel like a princess[34]. My worries melted away for a day and there was not a moment's hesitation before I said, "Yes."

About 11 months later, we both said: "I do." In that time, I was so happy I went off medication, thinking if there was a cure, this would be it. Marriage means happily ever after, right? I am cured! How even…

Permitting Myself to Create

Severe depression[35] isn't like chicken pox — you can get it more than once. And I did. The second time, in 2017, proved to be just as bad, if not worse. I recognized when I started spiraling again but I was stubborn, I refused to go get help, insisting that I could just push through it.

I decided all I truly needed to feel less empty was to "shake things up." I left secure job I enjoyed in favor of a startup. Six months into that decision, the long hours and lack of structure common in newer companies took their toll on me. I knew others did such jobs all the time, which just compounded my frustrations with myself. By the time I was ready to care for myself, however, the company explained that it could not accommodate my request to take time off once a week to see a doctor. I told myself things like "I am not a quitter," and "I don't really need to see a doctor," to force myself past it all. I went back to my therapist a few times for the rare weekend appointment she had, but I wasn't honest.

---

[34] *https://medium.com/@mxiety.marie/how-disneys-tangled-inspired-me-e487e43fec3e*
[35] *https://www.nimh.nih.gov/health/topics/depression/index.shtml*

I wanted to be strong, which meant going to therapy and venting out my anger without working on anything.

This anger fostered a realization. I imagined that there were other people out there who felt trapped inside of their minds, in jobs that did not permit the flexibility needed to maintain good mental health. I started writing about my experience as a way to cope, partly due to being lucky and finding a fantastic editor, and partly because I was tired of telling myself I didn't deserve to do things I knew would help me feel better.

Finally, one evening during a yoga retreat a word came to me, a pseudonym: Mxiety (Marie/Anxiety). With this I had the cover I needed to publicly confront the emotional strain I felt trying to maintain my identity past my mental illness. I realized that I was ready to talk about what was going on inside, to fight the internal and external dialogue telling me I had to keep it all hidden.

Around this time, I also suffered a debilitating panic attack at work. A full crying breakdown, in front of my colleagues and bosses. It was agreed that it would be best if I took time off my job. Indefinitely.

I decided that moment was my "now-or-never". Either I accepted defeat from my mental illness or I finally gave back, as I promised myself I would. With newly available time, I created my website[36] and set up conversations via live stream to help others in real time. The resulting show, writing, and activism facilitated a community and fulfilling connections in ways I didn't know I needed. There is now a small network[37] of people who support each other via live chat and offline that I brought together. My goal was to put information out there to fill the gap I found when I needed help: reliable, researched

---

[36] *https://mxiety.com/*

[37] *http://twitch.tv/mxiety - http://Mixer.com/mxiety*

discussions on mental illness. The achievement became so much bigger than the goal.

There's been so much progress made. I am writing here, giving myself credit for both those things. That used to be near impossible. My now husband supports me just as he did before, but I am in a better place to support him too. The floodgates are open and now there is no pushing back my creative aspirations. All of this is not enough to remove scary thoughts completely, but it's enough to feel empowered to hold them back.

I dedicate this final paragraph to that ugly creature which remains in my head. You may darken my achievements with your presence, but you are never winning. There is too much unknown in my future to give into your ideas. I am sure there are worse things ahead because I have seen them before. But I am equally sure that the good things can outshine those awful things. If you're going to keep rummaging, I have to keep fighting. I wish I could get rid of you once and for all, but as long as you are here to stay, to keep me down, I resolve to keep you down.

I'm Not Okay and That's Not Okay

SOME WEEKS ARE BETTER THAN OTHERS. Some weeks I feel empty inside. So emotionless, so exhausted from hearing my own belligerent thoughts, that it seems dying would be a better alternative to continuing life with the emotions I currently feel trapped in. It's not right, but it's what I am hearing as I go through my day to day activities.

And that's not okay.

Let me clarify, it's okay that I am not okay. Okay to accept I am not perfect. Continuing to pretend like I'm strong so that no one should doubt my capabilities, pretending I am inhuman so I can continue keeping up an appearance — it only lasts so long. I did so at two jobs in my career. In one scenario, I ended up crying in the supply closet daily. In another, I had a very public panic attack, in a moment when I didn't steal enough time to get to the bathroom and hide it there.

Up until those moments, even though I had discussions with my co-workers about my not feeling well, no one really thought anything was wrong. I made every meeting even though in the mornings I had to force myself out of bed. I did my makeup and hair and kept up appearances well. So well, I thought I could even fool myself. I didn't know it was okay that I was going through a hard time because no one around me talked about it, and that's not okay.

It's not okay to get yourself so overworked that you feel too trapped to continue with life. There is so much to experience: from the monotony of day-to-day life to the extraordinary moments like weddings or births.

Feeling this way, or lacking feeling in this way, did not make me less of anything, nor really that weird. 16 million adults[38] (6.9 percent of adults) experience a major depressive episode in a year. And the number 1 in 5 gets thrown out so often, I almost don't need to cite it.

It's not okay that there is a whole generation, my generation, of people experiencing similar symptoms in unprecedented numbers. In part, arguably due to an economy[39] that left us unable to match our parent's accomplishments, and in part because we're coming up to an era where we have started to admit mental health is as important as physical health.

I hear my contemporaries use the words[40] "burn out," and "lazy" together in a self-deprecating way and I cringe. It's the mark of being told most of your life that you are ungrateful and have it so well in a world that is "your oyster" only to find out that the previous generation doesn't care to mentor you, so you have no idea how to properly shuck it.

What's not okay, is the social trophy[41] you get for overextending yourself. I write, have a podcast, work full time and teach yoga, and every moment I am not doing those things I am considering what a waste of space I am. That is until I feel the aforementioned "burn out" and can barely put thoughts together without bursting into tears. At that moment and for the next maybe week or so I give myself permission to breathe and then I restart the race against my own sanity again.

It's not okay that I feel like I am not living up to a personal expectation and it's not okay that my contemporaries might internally compare themselves to me through the social media[42] that I am forced to keep up because

---

[38] *https://www.nami.org/learn-more/mental-health-by-the-numbers*
[39] *https://www.npr.org/2018/01/07/576301190/millennials-and-the-economy*
[40] *https://humanparts.medium.com/why-do-all-my-friends-want-to-kill-themselves-cd0f21609ee6*
[41] *https://www.gallup.com/workplace/237377/millennials-burning.aspx*
[42] *https://journals.plos.org/plosone/article?id=10.1371/journal.pone.0069841*

otherwise no one would know that I am writing, podcasting, working full time and teaching yoga all at the same time.

It's not okay that I am constantly not ok.

At my worst moments I have spent 6 hours a week getting to, from and sitting with my therapist and then psychiatrist to maintain my sanity. I love my doctors, I really do, because they ensure that I do not crumble into a pile of tired, emotionless, suicidal dust. But the only thing worse than all the time I have had to spend with them to get myself healthy, is that in 2017, 12.2 percent could not afford to spend time or money on doing the same.[43]

It's not okay, or rather, it's not fair.

I had to learn that it's okay not to be okay, and, re-learn it after I took myself off of medication because people around me told me I should be scared to be on it. I was not okay without medication and am grateful that I found a very small community of people who gave me the emotional approval I needed in order to keep myself on it without feeling broken or less of a capable person.

I take full responsibility for the fact that I let a relative's judgmental look decide whether I could continue freelancing. I let that get to me. I do not expect nor want to be coddled, but it's not fair that I grew up[44] in a manner that made me seek approval from others whenever I need to make a life changing choice. It's unfair but it's also no one else's problem.

It's not okay that I have lived a life which makes me have to take a deep breath and remind myself that it's okay not to be okay. It's not okay that I ever have felt suicidal

---

[43] *https://www.reuters.com/article/us-usa-healthcare-uninsured/u-s-healthcare-uninsured-rises-most-in-near-decade-gallup-idUSKBN1F5230*
[44] *https://medium.com/@mxiety.marie/what-i-learned-about-forgiveness-through-my-abusive-parents-8bd49dadf4e7*

because it means pieces of my life have brought me to that moment.

What's most important is to give yourself permission to get better. So that you're "not okay" turns into an "okay".

The reason that hashtag #itsoktonotbeokay even took off is because of how intent we are on pushing ourselves past our breaking point. We won't admit that we need help even though we feel like we're drowning. Gender, sex, country of origin, socio-economic status and race only multiply the issue. And none of that is okay.

3 Reasons Friendships with People Who Have Depression Are Incredible

LIKE ANY PERSON YOU MIGHT KNOW, I've been hurt by other people. Particularly memorable experiences get thrown into my baggage, to be carried until some unforeseen moment. Now, having collected enough knick-knacks in past relationships, unsure what to do with them, I have started a lot of my recent new encounters by boldly opening up the bag and showing off a particular piece to gauge reactions.

At times, I just can't help it — I forget to distill my past experiences and express only the "more palatable" ones. It's not the best gauge of character for the person I meet, and can be rather unfair from my end to do so. Despite all of that, if I don't see clues of **"fight or flight"**[45] kicking in, sometimes I can make a new friend because a very special type of connection is forged.

The contents of my baggage are often tied to my mental illness in one way or another. Likely, because **our empathy is best engaged**[46] whenever we recognize an emotion we ourselves have gone through, I have found that those who carry similar pieces, or symptoms, are always the kinder and more forgiving. They've been more patient when I have to explain my irrational behavior and less judgmental about the life choices I have to make to avoid triggers or something similar. Overall, they're just incredible people who make me feel like I belong.

---

[45] *https://science.howstuffworks.com/life/inside-the-mind/emotions/fear2.htm*
[46] *https://nyaspubs.onlinelibrary.wiley.com/doi/pdf/10.1111/j.1749-6632.2009.04418.x*

They're "giving people" to a fault.
As with any long-term condition, although I would hope it doesn't define us, mental illness affects most aspects of life. It's no small point to note that people who have lived experience with depression, for example, are more likely treat my knick-knacks gently, almost as if they were their own. So many fellow people with depression are the kind of people who, although depressed themselves, carry an antiseptic and bandages in case their friend, whom they've seen self-harm before, relapses. They are the kind of person who will reach out and listen to you discuss your tough day, though they might not be having the best one either. It's no coincidence either that I am often offered love and care with no expectation of a return. I know it's in part because helping others **has been proven**[47] to help ourselves, but it's also because we know how it feels to live with something outwardly inexplicable and invisible.

They're often empaths.
I wouldn't wish being an empath upon anyone, but this makes this trait in others all the more valuable to me. Having empathy means when I come to that person with a complaint or a worry, they will respond as though it is theirs, the way they would hope someone would treat them when they've felt similar emotions. There are certainly those whose **depression made them feel empty**[48] — those who have had to re-learn emotions. And I have seen even those people offer more moral support to someone suffering than someone who has enjoyed a fairly uneventful life overall.

---

[47] *https://psycnet.apa.org/doiLanding?doi=10.1037%2Femo0000178*
[48] *https://themighty.com/2018/05/depression-i-feel-empty/*

Emotional hyper-awareness.
I will say 9 out of 10 of those who have also lived through a mental illness have more to offer emotionally. Someone who has confronted their depression instead of repressing it will be unlikely to ask you to repress your emotions. Indeed, they might prefer to dissect them instead. They will study them just like you do. Questions like, "why do you think this is happening," "is this triggering a memory you don't like," "do you need to talk about it," and my favorite, "isn't it interesting how people…" will come out of their mouths.

One of my closest current friends described exactly this quality as a reason she wanted to spend so much time with me. It was as though she always watched the world from the sidelines and just now learned there are others watching from the same angle, while the rest of the world seems to be able to fully experience a wide range of emotional understanding without such observation.

I am not implying there is a league of nice people who are made such solely because they have a mental illness. I don't want to encourage a victim-type mentality in order to gain friends. However, I have made new **friends through having this common issue**[49], and have strengthened my relationships with old ones by opening up on this topic.

Look into your bag. If you carry similar items, take a moment. Consider their usefulness and beauty before you permit your mind to discount their value to others. Depression might be a type of baggage, but it's one that makes for some incredible bonds with exceptional people.

---

[49] *https://themighty.com/2017/05/best-friend-has-depression/*

What Being Inside a Flashback Is Like for Someone With PTSD

HERE'S THE THING ABOUT FLASHBACKS: it's not like the movies. There is no darkness, swirling lights, no feeling of falling through a tunnel, no stars floating by or potions that read "drink me." One moment I am in the present, typing on keys, writing this. The next, I am on the floor of my closet crying and trying to hurt myself.

The scene was horrible the first time around. Reliving it again is like being trapped in a nightmare and not being able to tell if you've woken up. And that's exactly the experience. The reality I am in, in a flash, is replaced by a new reality created from a memory.

Let me back up. Have you seen *Inside Out*?[50] Don't worry if you haven't, I won't spoil the important stuff. Just that it has this great way of explaining what memories are. Imagine a big storage case, with a ton of clips sitting inside and when you recall one, your brain works like a vending machine to dispense it to your consciousness.

Well, with flashbacks — or in my case, **post-traumatic stress disorder**[51] — the vending machine is broken and releases too many clips out at once, or starts dispensing them without someone placing an order, at the wrong time. Anything I have lived through can be easily accessed at any moment. Good or bad memories, the brain is dispensing without regard.

You know that feeling you get when you see the first snow hit the ground on Christmas Day? That's your brain taking an amalgamation of all the positive things you

---

[50] *https://movies.disney.com/inside-out*
[51] *https://www.nimh.nih.gov/health/topics/post-traumatic-stress-disorder-ptsd/index.shtml*

associate with Christmas and giving them to you as you encounter the situation again, making you feel good.

PTSD is usually a sign that a lot of traumatic memories have been stored. They can be released by encountering triggers. A **flashback trigger**[52] **is anything** in the surrounding environment that dispenses a relevant memory to be relived. Remember how, in the TV show *Scrubs*, J.D. **would have daydreams** after someone would describe a scenario? He would literally picture it and then have to be snapped out of it.[53]

How about when you smell perfume and remember something nice about your mom who wore the same scent? Now imagine if, when you encountered that smell, you felt like you were physically back at the park she took you to, but you can't distinguish that memory from the reality you are in. Maybe, at the time, you fell and scraped your knee. Someone without PTSD can think of that memory and move on. Maybe get a bit upset, but move on. With PTSD, you can again feel the heat of the wound, and taste the salty tears on your cheeks. When this happens to me, I cannot distinguish that I am not hurt all over again.

My brain skews the perception of the world around me and I truly believe it is happening again. That's not easy to come back from. Another challenge to coming back is how colorfully my mind recalls the event. Twelve years ago, when the above-mentioned event was unfolding, I went into the closet because I wanted to pretend I wasn't in a home where someone was yelling and coming to hurt me. For this memory, the flashback is armed in threefold to trick me to stay:

1. I am scared because I feel like I am back in the closet.

---

[52] *https://themighty.com/2018/06/complex-post-traumatic-stress-disorder-ptsd-trigger-help/*
[53] *https://scrubs.fandom.com/wiki/Fantasies*

2. I am sweating because the closet is hot.
3. I can feel the physical pain as I attempted to hurt myself.

That's why it takes a bit to snap back. I am not usually too aware of time. If I am lucky enough, I might have someone who knows me by my side. They'll notice I am zoning out and getting upset and will try to get my attention back to true reality.

In addition, flashbacks cause me to be unsure of where I am on my timeline. Am I really at the park? Am I really on the couch or walking into a store? It's like that moment in a dream, where you realize you are asleep and you are figuring out how to wake up, except you think there's a chance you're already awake. **I have to reassess** in order to come back to the present.[54]

It's *Doctor Who*[55] without the cool sidekick.

My current life is so much less traumatic that I have been able to spend the past five years working on feeling better. I have medications which work in conjunction with my efforts to keep the memory vending machine working properly, as much as possible.

I know certain things can trigger me to live through memories, but I am armed. I have a lovely dog I can walk outside when I need a distraction. I have a husband who can see the signs and talk me back to reality. I have gone through therapy so I don't have to avoid triggers too much. I am grateful to be armed and now able to embrace this piece of me, flashbacks and all.

---

[54] *https://themighty.com/2017/09/deal-cope-with-post-traumatic-stress-disorder-ptsd-flashbacks/*
[55] *https://www.bbc.co.uk/programmes/b006q2x0*

I Can't 'Snap Out' of Depression, but I'm Working on What I Can Control

FROM FIRSTHAND EXPERIENCE I can say the darkness depression[56] creates can feel all-consuming. If you have gone through it, you have also undoubtedly experienced interactions with other people who can't comprehend how bad that space is.[57] Someone has inevitably recommended that you focus on all the "good things" you have or suggested perhaps you just need to change things up a bit. I have also heard I just needed to drink more water or start exercising.

And those people are not *entirely* wrong.

I was forced to confront the power that negative thought patterns had on me when, recently, I was obsessing over how many negative experiences I've had in my life. I recognized part of the reason I was miserable is that in recent years I felt like I had not had any positive experiences. Which, just statistically speaking, couldn't be true.

Something must have been positive? But had I put in any effort to recognize when those moments were happening? Or was I too afraid things could get worse in any moment, that I never stopped to appreciate the positive aspect of the moment and just enjoy it?

It was so much easier just to sulk and talk about the worst parts of my day, and eventually, that colored all of my experiences — even the ones that were not inherently bad.

If you focus on the negative and avoid any information that might potentially prove your current worldview wrong, you are actively avoiding potential change, positive and negative. That keeps you only in the

---

[56] *https://themighty.com/topic/depression/*
[57] *https://themighty.com/2018/09/what-you-shouldnt-say-to-someone-with-depression-alternatives/*

bubble of what you know. And since what I know was primarily based on negative experiences, the chances of suddenly thinking differently were obviously super slim.

Here is the issue though: how do you get yourself out of your bubble and into a broader worldview? At the moment, in that persistent darkness, it is all you know, and so it will likely be the pattern you continue to follow.

I am not here to argue that people should stop trying to help those with mental illnesses unless "they've lived through it themselves." Nor will I discount the impact a more positive outlook can have on someone's quality of life. The issue is the assumption that depression comes to be by way of choice.

I want to be happy, but I also need to accept my limitations as a chronically depressed person, the same way someone with **arthritis**[58] might accept theirs. Life is still going to be awesome, but I have had to actively talk myself out of having suicidal thoughts and am constantly practicing Cognitive Behavioral Therapy techniques that most people never consider in through the course of their lives.

Pulling yourself by your bootstraps is even more impossible when you are depressed because depression implies a lack of straps altogether. And possibly boots.

It's not that the person is giving into the feeling of being upset, it's more about the **lack of feeling at all**,[59] and sometimes, not being able to understand or remember what feelings are altogether.

Positive thinking will work just about the same on a depressed person as the reverse would work on a cheerful person. Forcing me to feel happy or to get out of bed when I am not doing well will only set a spotlight onto the fact that it hurts to get up. It makes me think about *all* the other things

---

[58] *https://themighty.com/topic/arthritis/*
[59] *https://themighty.com/2018/09/i-feel-numb/*

I am not doing well enough (laughing, being a good friend, being someone who takes a shower) and will inevitably, 10 times out of 10, make me feel worse.

I am not cured or always happy just because I learned to see the world brighter. What I do know is that this change in perspective is definitely helping me lead a more satisfying life. I am open to continuing to receive that different perspective through therapy, medication and reading recent research.

Darkness might be relative to each person's experience, but staying inside of that headspace is often not up to us. What we can, and should, control is pushing ourselves outside of our minds. Not settling for the awful way we might be feeling and searching for ways to improve our lives. This means continuing the pursuit of what it means to be human, working to be your best self at all times.

Why Does Social Media Upset Us and What Can We Do?

IT SEEMS HARD TO ACCEPT that our lives are not perfect. That anything less than excellence is not only acceptable, but much more realistic. Spend just a few minutes on Instagram, and it seems everyone is eating the perfect lunch, wearing the perfect outfit, and living with the perfect family. Everyone except you of course. You can then presume that your life must be boring and pathetic because there are not enough social media-worthy moments in it.

And who can blame those picture-perfect Instagram models for posting their perfect pictures online for all to see? I certainly prefer to look at attractive people and nice, eye-catching images. The rest of the world is dull and grey, so seeing someone else look bright adds color to the moment, if nothing else. I am also aware of what the food I cook actually looks like—usually a cooked version of whatever I put in—so someone arranging their meal nicely is also a welcome sight for sore eyes.

There's a lot of things that are inarguably good about social media too. I have made meaningful connections in growing pockets of supportive online communities with so many wonderful people. To me, the social aspect of social media seems to be working just fine. The media part? Not so much.

Acknowledging The Problem

We've gotten to the point where the attitude of hiding problems[60] in favor of a perfect picture is feeding into the

---

[60] *https://www.scientificamerican.com/article/negative-emotions-key-well-being/*

already global mental health problem[61]. As a result, we have people who look like shining examples of happy humans breaking down, and even ending their own lives—renowned designer Kate Spade or famous chef Anthony Bourdain come to mind.

Talking about something such as depression marks you as "attention seeking." As though unhappiness is a burden that can be passed down. Never mind that, by definition, all social media posts are all attention seeking. So much so, that we get overwhelmed[62] giving that attention as often as our feeds refresh.

I have often found myself mindlessly scrolling, not even thinking about which posts I am hitting 'like' on. Other times I get sucked in and feel like am actively involved in other people's personal lives, often strangers. All without taking a moment to check in with how I am feeling amongst all of this comparison, that is until I start feeling absolutely terrible about myself.

If I am feeling ok, I don't mind seeing prettier-than-life things, in fact, I often feel they inspire me. However, if I am a bit down on myself already, the fire gets worse from the added coal of upward comparison. Is that anyone else's fault? Not exactly, I am the one who keeps scrolling.

I compare myself enough to people in real life, that confronting more things I am bad at online becomes downright exhausting. And according to some research, I know I am not the only one.[63]

---

[61] *https://thefederalist.com/2017/11/08/experience-postpartum-depression-will-help-understand-americas-mental-health-crisis/*

[62] *https://elemental.medium.com/why-your-brain-needs-idle-time-e5d90b0ef1df*

[63] *http://www.csus.edu/faculty/m/fred.molitor/docs/social%20networking%20and%20depression.pdf*

Understand the Time That Goes Into Each Post

Sure, I know that the person taking a picture of their dinner should be enjoying the moment, savoring the flavor of the meal, not spending time lining up the shot until the food gets cold. You've have seen it before, fork in one hand, perhaps sitting in front of a date, looking only at a phone screen while thinking about funny hashtags as their image uploads.

Will the meal really be enjoyed more by the people viewing the picture? On the other end, it usually takes me about 3 seconds to look at the image before I keep scrolling. Meanwhile, that person has spent precious time posting it, focusing on what others will think.

I know all of this, so why do I still get envious?

I forget that what I find interesting has been carefully curated, constructed to display the image that person wants to put out to the world.

On the surface I know that the picture of someone's expensive dinner was super staged. I can also imagine how silly they looked as they waited to take a bite until the incredible photo-op was complete. They stopped eating, just to snap a shot for people to see instead of being there, present in the moment. Yet, I cannot stop my mind from wondering why I am not the one enjoying time outside with my friends (whom the poster seems to have endless amounts of, by the way).

I try to refocus and remember.

Know That This Is Just a Moment

Ever been in the middle of an argument when someone asked to take a photo of the group? Ever spent a ridiculous amount of time picking out an outfit, only to spill sauce on it right before someone took a shot? You have stopped whatever it was you were occupied with to smile for the camera. You may have even hugged someone you don't enjoy spending time with for Instagram. In that fleeting moment, everything appears to be perfect.

That's the moment that will appear in people's feeds. That is what you are seeing in yours.

Stay in Your Lane
Social media might make us feel bad about ourselves, but we've noted that it also brings a lot of good into the world, as it's connected more people than it's hurt. Besides, you might argue, recent long-term studies have shown that social media has little to no effect on teenagers who are constantly exposed to screens.[64]

Where does that leave those of us who end up feeling awful? What do we do?

The only thing that works for me is grounding—reminding myself where I am, who I am and what truly matters to me in that moment. You can name three things surrounding you, or think of three things you did well that day, or just take a moment to look around yourself. You are one person, with only so much time and attention to offer the world.

It might also be time to clean up your feed and leave only accounts which have a positive impact on your mental state, whomever that might be.

The final key is to remember to **stay in your lane**. Focus on you. Nothing upward of who you need to be, nothing downward of what you fear you will become. Think about where you are in that moment. You. Just be you and stay in that moment. Even if you have a pimple you may need to photoshop out later.

---

[64] *https://www.bbc.com/news/health-48147378*

How I Stopped Comparing Myself to Others and Decided I Was Good Enough

I AM SURE THERE ARE PLENTY OF REASONS people are hard on themselves. My, unburdened by proof or research life-experience-based hypothesis has been that society is set up in such a manner that we are constantly seeking the next, more significant and shinier thing. Too often I have found that I feel content, only to freak out that I have become complacent and will then never amount to anything else. I go between, "shouldn't I want the bigger house?" to "wow, I am so happy to have everything I do, this is good and plenty" back and forth, repeatedly, almost daily.

But before I blame society as a whole, I consider the fact that my family also heavily reinforced these notions within me. If I said something like, "I was nervous I wouldn't do well on that test, but I ended up with a *B+*," I would usually get lectured as to why it was more important for me to stay focused on getting the perfect grade. And there is value to that, just not when someone is coming to you looking for an extra nudge of support.

Based on the amount of reading and studying I did and how long I spent at the library as a student, there was never a reason to think I wasn't aiming for that *A*. My parents were just bad at paying attention,[65] however, and they didn't know how anxious their words were actually making me. I craved a pat on the shoulder for the *B*, but they wanted that trophy so that they maintained bragging rights in front of family and friends.

---

[65] *https://mxiety.com/blog/what-i-learned-about-forgiveness-through-my-abusive-parents?rq=abusive*

As a result, there was no room to learn what would make me happy. No place to find out what kind of person I was outside of the accomplishments I chased. No time to spend on something silly like that. All of my time needed to be spent finding and then chasing the next thing. Each time I got closer to it, I was reminded that there was nothing I could do to actually reach some sort of final destination. As if that existed.

During my early twenties, I recognized that I spent so much time running after a carrot on a stick, I began to wonder if it was okay to blame my family for this endlessly tired but insanely driven person I had become.

What became clear more than anything else is that my thirst for validation was running the show—anything that could fill the void that an empty participation trophy used to take up.

So, what did I do?
I let myself hit the wall of admitting that "I actually have no idea what I am doing" and proceeded in threefold:
- Accepted that I am not the things my parents told me I needed to be
- I was more than a grade and not a prize horse, and I was a living human being outside of my achievements.
- Accepted my limitations
- I wouldn't win every time, and that's okay.
- In times when I don't feel well, I spent time finding what I enjoyed.

I used to push harder and harder until I would break down crying exhausted. I wanted to stop chasing my tail, and instead, use all of that pent-up frustration to start the journey towards finding who I was.

So What Action Did I Take?

First, I set up some long-term goals. These were loose and a bit broad like a bucket list for the rest of my life. I want to be a published writer, I want to devote my career to helping others feel less of the sting of mental illness stigma, and maybe have a child.

All of these were choices I made based on where I wanted my life to go; life, fully controlled by me. In comparison, seeking my parent's appreciation created a goal I had little control over. It was not contingent on my hard work, but rather their feelings at any given moment. From that point, all of my future actions would be moving to fulfill a purpose that I establish. There was still a proverbial carrot on a stick, but I got to determine the length of the stick and in which cases I would be allowed to just grab it and eat it.

By setting up long term personal goals, I helped myself re-direct bad habits, and I gave myself a clear purpose. Whenever I would start having depressive thoughts about what I had not yet done, I could remind myself of that purpose, ensuring that I kept focusing on it long term and away from how many re-tweets, website visits or live stream viewers I didn't get.

Now, the hardest part has been maintaining my goals in the ever-shifting sands of early 20s life changes. I suppose the actual difficulty was accepting that sometimes I would need to roll with the punches, and most importantly, recognize that not every single thing I do would validate me in some way. And that, is more than just okay.

The Reality of Loving Someone with Mental Illness

WHEN THINGS SUDDENLY FIT TOGETHER, life feels like a romantic comedy cliché. Two nerdy kids go out on a date after being introduced by a mutual friend. There's the ingénue who's expressed to her friends that she's "not looking to date" so she can "figure herself out". In comes the love interest with green eyes and a mop of fluffy brown hair who is able to complete all of her sentences.

On their first date, they find out they both know what it feels like to be trapped inside of one's mind. One of them was diagnosed and had been told by a doctor this means he was dealing with a mental illness. He describes how lonely he feels, like no one quite gets where his pain is coming from. She understands. She tells him how she wishes she could make it all better for him. She admits she could use a doctor as well.

Her hand is by her side on the cold ground. He puts his hand on hers without looking at her. They both feel safe. Then they walk and have their first kiss by the lake, at sunset, where birds take flight as the two embrace. They get married eight years later and all is well.

Actually.
There is no third person narration. There is no romance in suffering, even if it is together. But boy, isn't it a pretty snapshot from my life. Two real people met as they were dealing with personal internal pain and without promising to *fix* each other, they helped each other through it.

After they kissed, they noticed how cold it was outside and stopped by a nearby Starbucks. They both grabbed a drink and a comfy seat. The reality is, about an hour later, they very diplomatically agreed that dating might be a good idea. I quote:

"It seems we are quite compatible, I don't see why we wouldn't try dating," he noted.

"I've never met someone looking for the same thing as I at our age. Indeed, worst case, we can always just stop," she added.

If you continue in boring reality, and you meet her about three months later, you find her saying:

"I have decided that I will not end my life. I can't do that, knowing that there is a life I can build with you. It seems like there was nothing going for me before we met, but now that we have, I want to see this through. Not in a "I'll kill myself if you leave" kind of way, but a "you feel like fate" kind of way. And I am not about to argue with fate."

Manic pixie dream girl or candidate for codependency, you decide.

No, the real happy ending is when both work for themselves to become better for each other. Not as two halves of a whole, but rather as two almost whole pieces coming together to spark something completely new into being.

Real life is when you grow together, seek therapists, follow their advice until you feel better and then say:

"I promise I am going to get better for you, because this is more than I ever thought I would deserve and I am ready to let myself believe that I deserve love now."

Some people confuse *real life* to mean all the worst parts of being together: the arguments, the tiffs, the illness. I insist *real life* is just those day to day things. It's not dramatic one way or another. But there are also no butterflies in one's stomach when it comes to picking out which almond milk you should buy for the house—vanilla or plain—because you're both lactose intolerant. It's getting to the point where you both just **are who you are** and knowing that you both worked hard to achieve this normal, this real thing. Together.

How "Kingdom Hearts" Helped Me Through Mental Illness

WHAT STARTED AS A Square Enix alignment with a little-known[66] animation studio they shared an office building with, is now a giant, multi-decade franchise. In my personal experience, I have found there is a deeper reason that *Kingdom Hearts* (KH) and its defenders: Sora, Donald, Goofy, Riku, Kairi and others, have won the hearts of gamers across the globe.

As a kid, I never owned a PlayStation. My family's budget priorities never included a game console after they bought the Nintendo Entertainment System on sale in 1992. Having always been a huge Dis-nerd, as soon as I heard about *Kingdom Hearts*, I was dying to see it. This was also the peak of my chain-wearing phase, so, the protagonist and I had a lot in common. I ended up watching my friends play it, being also too self-conscious about my poor reflexes to dare try playing myself.

Of course, I wasn't disappointed with what I saw, *Kingdom Hearts* created a rich world of its own and gave 'good vs evil' another dimension by layering it atop the 'dark vs light' battle. And that battle, thanks to a bit of time hopping, memory wiping, and Heartless lore, evolves into the battle we have with literal alternate pieces of ourselves.

When I was 19, I was diagnosed with anxiety, depression, and obsessive-compulsive disorder with post-traumatic stress disorder. Long story short, by 27 my mental health was so poor that I had to leave the professional work environment for a bit. Wanting to make the best of an awful situation, I started an IRL (in real life themed) Twitch channel

---

[66] *https://www.youtube.com/watch?v=VN24JkNKJiA*

dedicated to educating others about the cause. I started playing *Stardew Valley* on stream but one day I mentioned that I had dreamed of playing *Kingdom Hearts* since I was little. My community was all for it and was excited for me to embark on learning how to use a controller properly (none of that *Mortal Kombat* and *Smash Bros* button-mashing I had been practicing). My husband, a gamer since he was six, promised patience, and after finding a great deal on a PS4, we took off.

I was re-enchanted by the Disney characters from the first second—but as an adult, I noticed more of their complexity and commitment to persevering in tough situations, whether they found themselves with friends or alone.

There were many twists in my emotional journey as I embarked to complete the first game. For one I was terribly frustrated that my fingers were not working as quickly as my mind was processing on-screen information (my husband still teases me for screaming "MAGIC" at the top of my lungs at an approaching enemy instead of pressing the appropriate buttons). By the end of the thirty hours it took to finish just the first game, I was blown away by how deeply I connected with all of the characters' mental turmoil as it surfaced through their decisions.

Fighting Against the Unseen
The evil beings for most of the game are called, quite descriptively, Heartless. Personifying darkness, they run amok and are constantly trying to take over and hurt the protagonist. The main villain, Xehanort, is hellbent on creating a world full of darkness at any cost. In my mind, both of these are a great personification of depression. It's aimless, everywhere, and will take over if you don't actively fight it.

These Heartless, along with other Disney villains, and Xehanort, do well to keep Sora and his friends—love interest Kairi and best friend Riku—apart.

I have found that depressive symptoms, such as lack of emotion and apathy, can feel personal to those who have never experienced it before. It's hard to understand that there is an evil Xehanort-like voice in my mind saying things to keep me low and too scared to turn to others for help. As a result, my relationships have always been rather strained, creating rifts between family members and friends and me. And after hearing so much negative self-talk all the time, how could you permit anyone to stay close?

As a result, I have lost quite a few friendships. I have had friends like Riku, who misconstrued Sora's disappearance to fight against the darkness as a personal slight. Even worse, without his friend, Riku succumbed to the darkness himself. He does so to both connect with Sora and because he knows it is so within reach for him. His emotional journey through the series includes pushing others away, although he does desire to save them in the end. He feels like he has to sacrifice himself for others to be fulfilled. I liken this to withdrawing from friendships because depression lets you believe you are less capable than others or worse, I often believed I didn't deserve friends.

> *"This world is perfect for me. If this is what the world really is...just this, then maybe I should fade back into darkness."* Riku, Kingdom Hearts 2.5.

You Never Win Against Depression Alone

For many of us, mental illness becomes such a constant guest in our lives that we are forced to go seek new friendships with people who might understand it better. Sora finds these friends in Donald and Goofy, as those are the only beings who can truly comprehend the scope of his task, the darkness that lies ahead, and are willing to make the situation the best it can be in the process of overcoming it. During the worst of my illness, I found a community on Twitch which has now become a large support group, assisting each other through personal ups and downs. Like Hercules in *Kingdom Hearts 2.5* we may have hit rock bottom, but we really just need the right people to help us believe in ourselves again. Connecting with people and creating a community is what inspires others to open up, even if they may not have done so otherwise.

I started my gameplay feeling like Aqua at the end of *Birth By Sleep:* about to give up, considering fading *"into the darkness"*, but both of us were reminded that there are others fighting just as we are, and that helps us continue wanting to keep fighting and pushing through.

> *"Yeah, there's darkness inside me, just like you said. But darkness is my enemy! And you are, too, for making everything around here reek of it!"'* -Riku, Kingdom Hearts 2.5

You Can and Should Continue To Fight Depression
There was one final lesson I learned about the perception of mental illness that I truly felt may have been the most important. The worst advice I have heard time and again for handling mental illness is to buck up, which needless to say, is not helpful. I found that *Kingdom Hearts* approached this with a refreshing angle. When I first watched Donald tell Sora the conditions of his companionship I was upset: "… You can't come along looking like that. Understand? No frowning. No sad face. Okay?" Sora had just lost his friends and wasn't sure he would ever see them again. I know it's just a game, but while I was not feeling well, I didn't need one of my favorite Disney characters telling me I wasn't welcome unless I was faking joy.

What I've learned this actually means in the lore of this game, is that walking around thinking of how unwell you are is not what gets you to your final goal. If you are truly unwell, you should stay at home, but if you can, consider the bigger picture at hand: what good could you be working on spreading?

Knowing that something did not end well and made us feel a certain way is never a guarantee that the future will hold the same. If we want to keep going forward, we have to take the attitude of going forward, taking our bouts of depression in stride as part of the road we've been put on. I ended the game realizing what Donald really meant was, we can't let our thoughts, our past, or our hurt, stop us. We must smile, but not so that others think we are ok, but so we remain hopeful that things can get better.

I write this the day before starting a new job in the professional world. Of course, I am not claiming that *Kingdom Hearts* "cured" my mental illnesses with its brilliant adventure and complex story-telling. What it did was put my mind at ease, as I saw my problems reflected in this story, one with incredibly brave heroes. Despite the hand they were dealt, they chose to continue putting others needs before their own, shining brighter and proudly while helping others.

Some will see these parallels as a stretch, many will think they oversimplify the story, but I think there are hundreds of people who are now smiling, believing and pushing forward, because Sora, Riku, Kairi, Terra, Aqua, Ventus, Donald and Goofy showed them how. I went to look for these parallels because I was looking for answers. The result, was that I was inspired to be the kind of person who also wants to keep fighting. I hope you are too.

A Year of Following My Purpose; AKA, You Are Not Alone When You're Live

I'M PRETTY SURE I actually teared up when I streamed one day back in October 2017, and not one person came for forty minutes. I was talking to myself while researching a mental health topic, but no one was there to care that I was doing so. I think I actually said out loud: "who cares if I'm here, I should just give up." Then, quietly, I resolved to keep researching, because I knew I would be doing the same thing if offline otherwise.

At that exact moment someone popped into my chat and asked me what I was doing. I talked about my research topic and how happy I was to see this person chat with me because without interaction, I was just talking to myself about medical diagnosis, which I found to be ironic to say the least. We both laughed a bit. That was just about a year ago as of this writing.

I've learned more about my self-worth and image over the past year than in the preceding twenty-seven. I have learned to see myself as a person before I see myself as a streamer or a writer, where before I thought that what you do *must* define you. I've learned that you can be more than you can ever define yourself to be, because while public perception is close to what you put out, it is also completely nuanced. I did not start streaming thinking this would be something I learn.

I've also found out that people interact with each other based on their personal emotions and assumptions. Every struggle, every day for each person, is theirs and theirs alone. Every comment, every word we speak has little to do with the person we are speaking to and everything to do with the ongoing battle in our consciousness (and subconscious selves, if you're into psychoanalytics).

Keeping all of that in mind, the one word that comes when I think of how to summarize it all, streaming, writing and discussing mental health online is: **Community**.

This has also been discussed ad nauseum as it is the cornerstone of Twitch, but from October to October, it's the one thing that connects it all. Who reads my writing? My community. Who understands what my dysphoria truly feel like? My community. I started the project telling my husband: "If I cannot help just one person during every episode and with every piece of my writing, I will quit. But all I need to keep this up is one person." That count's a bit higher than one today, and I am grateful beyond words.

I frequently say that Mxiety is an idea of hope, which is bigger than the person who started it or any one person who supports it. It's the belief that since we live in a time when the world doesn't know how to feel about mental illness, it's up to us to show them and take care of each other when no one else knows how. It what created *Be The Light* as our sign off.

Just over twelve months ago, I felt alone and scared, like no one was listening even though I was surrounded by all the love my incredible husband and friends could offer. I felt stupid, yet angry, and most of all, I felt like I needed some kind of purpose. Maybe if I let others know what I knew, I could make them feel like this less often. And, I just wanted to stop seeing people with mental illness misunderstood and mistreated because of things they had little control over.

Never in my wildest dreams, when I sat sobbing three years ago on the floor of my bathroom, wishing I could die, did I ever realize that I could incubate a whole community. When I was driving and talking myself into not ending my life, I could not fathom the number of people who had done exactly the same and were looking for someone to tell them they are not alone. I thought of making something like Mxiety, but in that moment all of those people I *could be helping* were faceless and nameless, just me working behind the scenes to help someone.

I know I found some version of a calling, when I noticed that I would not shut up when someone asked me what I could do if I could start anything. I would launch into detail about my plans for a website, a live-stream, and *finally* getting myself to write consistently.

It took a community of like-minded people to confirm to me, beyond a doubt, that there is a friend out there on the internet for all of us. That people want to help each other, especially those whose hardship was invisible. Seeing others like them made them finally feel as special as every one of us wants to feel in our lives.

These are no longer just "people out there with mental illness," but friends and kind humans who are willing to help others after knowing for years what being alone feels like. It became a group of people who work *every day* just to be a functioning version of themselves. They all have names, they all just want to be loved like anyone else and many of them (100+ as of January 2020) have given me the honor of sharing their story live on air.

Those who come back to read and see more inspire me to keep learning, keep pushing and keep trying, even though some days I am painfully reminded that I need more knowledge, more experience, more time and more ...everything else.

After listening to so many personal stories, I can conclude that while each of us lives a different life, which informs how we handle our hardships, the hardships themselves –the human experience — it's the same.

So, if you haven't yet, come share your story[67], because every single one of them matters, each one makes at least one person feel less alone. Doesn't matter if you have thousands of people following you online, or you work as an accountant, you too can be the light for others.

If you do currently follow me and are reading this because that's a thing you do, thank you, from the bottom of my heart, for taking the dream of a girl crying in her car and making me feel better than I ever thought I could. You have made my dream **a purpose**.

If you are struggling today, please don't end your journey on this earth with us. I know how bad it can hurt, but amidst that I found my passion. I believe you can get up and find yours. Or tell me to *F**k off*, what do I know?

---

[67] *https://mxiety.typeform.com/to/Xwpeho*

Science Reminds Me I Am Small, But I Need To 'Think Big'

DESPITE MY DEPRESSION, PTSD and anxiety, I am a naturally an easily excitable person. It's a telling trait to those who know me. I love the Muppets and Sailor Moon and Star Wars and most books and board games. But there is nothing I love more than science. Any time I notice stars in the sky while I am outside walking my dog in the evening, I am likely to stop dead in my tracks in awe.

The universe is vast, and as far as we know[68], it's only getting bigger. I understand that for some people, this is a terrifying prospect. If everything is so big, and we really live on nothing more than a pale blue dot[69], what could we possibly do that matters?

Well, For One, It Gives Me Purpose And Perspective.
Since we're so small, anything we try to do won't have a true impact unless it's ginormous. Meanwhile, for one reason or another, the negative things people do and say around us tend to feel huge. They become reminders of the falsity that we are small, with little to offer the world. To me, that just means that every hug, every confession of love needs to be bigger and bolder, so that all the negative things, such as fighting and anger, appear ever smaller.

The universe is dark, vast and scary. Sometimes just our planet feels terrifying and daunting, but that doesn't mean you're small or unimportant. It means that in your small corner, making a big difference in someone else's small corner matters even more.

---

[68] *https://www.nasa.gov/feature/goddard/2016/nasa-s-hubble-finds-universe-is-expanding-faster-than-expected*
[69] *https://www.planetary.org/explore/space-topics/earth/pale-blue-dot.html*

Your kind act might feel big to the person receiving it. It might be forgotten soon, because of how we understand time relative to those around us, but that's all the more reason to keep up your kind deeds. Then, lots of small yet generous acts over a period of time, lead to an overall big picture of positivity the same way a concentrated amount of negativity will do otherwise.

The universe is random, abiding by the law of entropy[70]. Take a moment to consider the odds of each of us coming into being. Perhaps then you will feel lucky, or better yet, inspired to make your time here memorable. Coming into being out of pure chaos is an enthralling notion — of all the tiny particles in the universe — **you became you.**

You are exactly as you biologically need to be, whatever that may be. With a disability, with some other perceived social stigma — there is no doubt that you have beaten the odds and the chaos to even come into existence.

Evolution[71] tells us that your ancestors survived and thrived for generations in order for each of us to come to be. When considering the chaos and the natural threats we have already overcome just within our species (both man-made and natural), the idea of taking my own life feels absolutely illogical, and maybe even kind of absurd. Suddenly, my worst thoughts, are *just* thoughts.

Space and science are what I perceive to be the few perpetual promotors of progress. Individual people, and in some cases, societies, might feel stagnant and regressive even. But science? Even when scientists are working on something that is unsuccessful or questionable, the teachable lesson is always implemented, and momentum is incrementally gained. Things like academic review and the

---

[70] *https://www.merriam-webster.com/dictionary/entropy*
[71] *https://www.startalkradio.net/category/evolution/*

scientific method inspire in my optimism, as they were set to ensure exactly such progress.

And So It Goes…
Light takes years to travel to us, and our planet is made up of stardust. Yet, it all comes together. Darkness takes light and absorbs it, which means more light is needed to continue to bring warmth and allow for life to exist. I see the big, dark, universe I am surrounded by as clearly as I see the small dark galaxy inside of my depressive mind and want to create light in both.

Looking out into the stars, I feel small. I know I have very little to do with what happens to me, yet somehow, it's all set for me to continue to evolve and create. I can do big things by working on the immediate small universe inside of me to ensure it gets used to positively affect my surroundings. I can let my fear go, knowing that by being small, a have the means to make something big.

It's truly, a relative perspective.

Following Your Dreams Won't Fix Everything, but Accepting Them Will

IT WAS THE SUMMER OF 2015, about three years before this writing. As I drove my car, I truly considered ending my life, picturing all the ways I could do it. I recall promising myself something cheesy, like "when I feel better, I will work to make sure no one ever feels this way." Little did I know I was not going to "get better" in any traditional sense. But I also didn't know I would have to pursue my passion in order to finally get onto a healthy path. By no means do I recommend getting to your worst before you finally chose to make things better for yourself.

I simply think it might be helpful for someone out there to know that listening to that small voice in the back of your head that does believe in you, while the rest of your body succumbs to depression, might be worth their while.

In a world where it feels like the news is getting worse every day; where so many of us day-dreamers are stuck sitting at an office desk with no windows; I can't help but smirk when I hear some celebrity advise me to just "follow your dreams." My dreams don't pay my bills and are the reason I am still forty-five thousand dollars in college debt. Not to mention, anytime I have attempted to entertain those dreams, I normally spiral into a panic about all the things that could go wrong, which in turn, has successfully kept me away from doing anything that wasn't immediately realistic. Until finally, I'd beaten myself into submission to follow a steady flow of income and just be content.

To this day, I insist that following your dreams is not what makes you happy anyway. **If happiness is the goal, then giving yourself permission to explore and finally act upon that small voice will more likely bring long-term joy.**

Chasing your wildest dreams is just not realistic for most of us. We need 401Ks, rent, and groceries, especially those of us who grew up without stability in those areas. But nurturing a smaller, more attainable piece of your biggest dream is very much within reach. Whether that's sitting down to write a poem for yourself, or going live when you play video games in your living room, doing something small can be incredibly fulfilling. It also helps you to continue pushing even if you are stuck in a job that makes you unhappy, just for the paycheck.

My dreams simmered on a low heat in my head until the constant bubbling became more exhausting and more taxing mentally to continue disregarding. Years of beating myself up for not being "good enough" "worthy of listening to" or, my favorite, "too much of a piece of garbage to do it," eventually took up so much of my headspace that it made it impossible for me to continue living. Again, I don't recommend waiting for it to get this bad before you do something.

The Relief of Letting Myself Be Was Palpable
Having finally given into the tiny voice that believed in me, has undoubtedly changed my life. It's given me more energy to write and have two jobs (one of which is full time) because I am not using precious brain bandwidth needed to even just tell myself that my life is worth living. I believe now that my dream was truly also my purpose, something that made my life distinct to me. It helped me understand how I should see myself in a sea of seven billion (and counting) people on the planet.

My worth, like that of many, was/is incorrectly tied to my work and my accomplishments. If out of 24 hours in a day, I had to spend 8 asleep and 18 awake, pushing myself to be the best at a job I didn't care for, I knew I couldn't last. Yet still I have given myself permission to follow what I want, the time I spent jobless and without a plan was just as stressful as keeping myself complacent with something I hated. Shitty catch 22 if you ask me, but as stressed as I am now juggling two things and a personal life, I am happier even though I am spread thin because I get to do what I love on top of a 9-5 I do not loathe.

I don't wish I started sooner even though I know that I am happier now.

You might note that in this essay, I have not mentioned what my dream was, because I find that irrelevant to getting anyone to be motivated about starting on theirs. Maybe even just figuring out what that might be. Starting work towards my dream was not easy and it took a lot out of me. Which is also why I would never advocate "just going for it." Doing that will never create as good of a result as spending hours getting the details you want to be proud of right. I knew my idea was bumpy and needed lots of polishing, but I was able to start on it because I was no longer a slave to my mind insisting I couldn't do anything. I could prove it wrong with my new actions—literally completing a task, checking it off and then knowing that I could continue and do it again.

Here are some other benefits I have found about following my dreams:
- I have found others who were passionate about the same thing; and some who were working on discovering if this passion we have in common would be something they could be pursuing further.
- My mental health is better because I can now affirm to myself that sometimes thoughts are *just thoughts*. I was able to push them away and *just act* instead, and that means I can do so again. I no longer have to keep

hypothesizing and being afraid, I know that *just doing it* works faster, even if I hit a few unexpected bumps.
- My personal life is richer for having more people in it, as my passion has brought out new aspects of my old friends, as much as it has helped me reach some incredible new ones.

The most difficult thing to commit to, believe it or not, is failure. It's hard to accept—it pulls on you, convincing you that you should just give up. It feels easy at first because it's all you know, but eventually, the weight of knowing you could have tried harder is too much to bear. Listen to that small voice in the back of your mind that believes in you, because it's too full of hope to smother and too tenacious to keep pushing away.

How Comparing Yourself to Others Is Worse Than Being Depressed

COMPARING MYSELF TO OTHERS has always been one of my talents. I've gotten to be pretty great at it. But just because we do it well, doesn't make it a great idea. Whether, I am thinking about how many readers or viewers I have or I'm simply unhappy with how my personal recovery compares to someone else's, the worst part about the practice is that I am very aware of how pointless it is. It's illogical. It's nonsensical. Without knowing fully why, I still fall into this trap.

I see on social media a rush to get higher numbers all the time. But we also can't fool ourselves into believing we don't enforce it offline as well. I am sure plenty of readers recall family members encouraging it: "See Bobby, listens to his mom, why can't you?" If you find your inner voice trivializing your personal experience in the light of what someone else is doing in similar ways, maybe it's time for us to reflect on this together. And no, you don't have to have actual depression[72] to feel the effects of this on your mental health.

We don't always punch up when we compare ourselves either. Sometimes, we compare ourselves to someone doing worse. Although at first glance this seems like a great way to feel better, it's really just another way to deny yourself appreciation of your own compliments, i.e. "So-and-so sucks and he has less followers than I do, at least I have more than him." Yep, feeling tons better. When we spend time being happy over *not being that guy* we are still creating an outside standard to go up against. Who is this person,

---

[72] *https://www.nimh.nih.gov/health/topics/depression/index.shtml*

what got them there, why did they fall so low? Maybe they're actually doing much better than they were yesterday. If you want others to respect that you're not always your best, time to start thinking about everyone surrounding you with the same lack of judgment.

I think we can all agree that continuously pushing up against an invisible, always stronger foe is probably not the greatest for our mental health. I know we can all agree that no one wins the comparison game. Not even the person who feels briefly better because they explained how their plight is worse than whatever it is you have to deal with.

The three ways that I repeatedly take my own validation is by reminding myself:
1. Someone is sicker than me
2. Someone deserves care and receives even less of it than I do
3. Someone deserves validation more than I do

The healthier thing to do would be to learn how to avoid this kind of thinking, altogether. And no, like everything else, we can't *just stop* doing it.

It's a tough thought loop to beat, but if it was easy I suppose I wouldn't be writing about it. Just like how I wouldn't be dwelling on *who is doing X better* if the necessity to do that wasn't so baked into our culture and nature.

A recent *New York Times* article (which included some great research)[73], talks about how being hard on ourselves was originally an incredibly useful trait for survival. It's a helpful motivator, it keeps us pushing, striving for more. However, for some people, that push becomes the only thing they can think about, and that's when we become our own obstacles instead of helpers.

---

[73] *https://www.nytimes.com/2018/05/22/smarter-living/why-you-should-stop-being-so-hard-on-yourself.html*

We create impossible goal posts that are likely to lead to disappointment, thus reinforcing the cycle of our not being good "enough" and creating insecurities around that. Usually these goals are external and largely out of our control. It's the difference between setting a goal of some number of followers over three days, versus setting a goal of walking outside for thirty minutes. One will actively give you endorphins and depends on your ability to choose to get up and start walking, whereas the other depends on other people doing something they may or may not do.

These comparisons win out not just due to our common DNA, but because they reinforce our belief that if we just work harder and reach something higher, we'll finally achieve happiness[74]. It's the idea that if we're not constantly moving the goal post, we must be lazy and unmotivated.

The thing is when you're depressed, having a goal of working towards recovery is already setting the bar high. That is no trivial thing. When you wake up every morning with the goal of simply not ending your life that day and setting out to have the best day possible, that's already beating odds[75]. Just not according to society because of how we trivialize mental health care. It's assumed to be a given. Assumed that you can just shake any issue off. Measuring your life against the high achievements of others is like a mouse measuring its height against an elephant. The mouse will never get there and has no idea that the elephant is terrified of the mouse's tiny presence as is.

Reaching towards goals that others have already accomplished is forgetting yourself. **Inherently that accomplishment (should you even reach it) will hold no perspective or meaning to you.** It's something someone else

---

[74] *https://www.amazon.com/Jaak-Panksepp/e/B001HD1O1S/ref=dp_byline_cont_book_1*
[75] *https://mxiety.com/blog/a-morning-with-mental-illness-an-open-letter*

has done. Without meaning there is no long-lasting value, hence why the pursuit will feel endless and fruitless.

Instead, it might be healthier to look to those who you envy as a source of inspiration. Change perspective in every sense. Sure, both inspiration and comparison are a means of doing something because someone else thinks it's important. But, should you choose to be inspired rather than compared, your achievement of the goal will be yours to be excited about. That's because instead of measuring up to another's success[76], you are using someone's ideas as a starting benchmark making them better, owning the process of making them yours.

It's like if Steve Jobs set out to make computers exactly the same as others and then got upset that no one wanted his product, which is exactly what everyone already owned. No, Steve Jobs saw a computer and set out to make it Macintosh.

What I do understand is the human need to be validated and how that plays into comparison game. First in the sense that we wish to be given credit when we're working hard to achieve something. It helps to stay motivated if you see that people outside of your situation think you're doing something great. That endorsement comes in the form of likes, claps, and hearts on social media.

Having myself watched a ton of videos on what to do and what to avoid to achieve X, there is nothing that deflates the ego more than following an influencer's advice and then seeing no change in your own status. No likes, no claps, no hearts, no follows. It's crushing. The more we do to be validated, the more we've been taught that we should be

---

[76] *https://www.quora.com/What-do-you-call-a-person-whos-always-pushing-themselves-to-get-better*

seeing results[77], the more that the herd, excuse me, other people, will show appreciation and validate us.

Secondly, it's hard to hear a story that evokes empathy when we haven't felt that empathy ourselves. The almost immediate light bulb that goes off in my head if I hear someone talking about their difficult childhood is that I want to share my story as well, as part of the story-telling exchange that we culturally come to expect. Worse, if the other person receives sympathy or help or really any of the things I was yearning for when I was telling my story, it becomes difficult not to resent them.

All of this said, the best thing that's helped me in this battle against comparison has been comparing myself to me. That way my hang-ups about my accomplishments are my own and any trends I see are easily traceable because I am the one who lived through them. Compared to last year's Marie, I am happier because I took my life back into my own hands and away from depression. When I've had a bad year, comparing myself to me won't feel as great, but it will keep me thinking about what I can do next to change that.

I use my realization that I am comparing myself to others as a signal, a bell to let me know it's time for self-reflection. Why did I need to look outside of myself? What about the person I am comparing myself to is something I envy/am self-conscious/am scared of? Now take that as a starting point and start working. Keep your nose to the ground to keep your trend upward. You can forget the rest. Your burden is heavy enough without adding someone else's accomplishments to it.

---

[77] *https://www.businessinsider.com/what-happens-to-your-brain-like-instagram-dopamine-2017-3*

How Accepting My Mental Illness Changed My Life

IT NEVER CAME AS A SURPRISE to me that I had depression. By now I have done the research and went through enough therapy to be certain, but even as a fourteen-year-old I was pretty sure there was something off about alternating between crying easily, but then being unable to experience emotions other than intense distaste for myself.

Thinking back, I didn't really fall apart until I was nineteen and starting college. I didn't have a lot of friends in high school. I didn't do any sports. At most I was editor of the yearbook club. I preferred to hang around with the teachers and took solace in reading and re-watching movies. When I did have encounters with kids my own age, I seemed to throw them off. Looking back, I am sure it was odd for them to see someone get off a phone call only to start hysterically crying because the person on the other end of the line just screamed at them for leaving the house without cleaning the toilet to their liking. Yes, specifically the toilet only. Those were the kind of calls I got from my family.

Back then I asked people often, "**What do you think of me? What kind of a person am I? A likable one? Is getting along with me hard?**" It shouldn't be surprising to know that people responded affirmatively often. It didn't help that I would always start crying.

Today, I am aware that I am in control of making myself into the kind of person I want to be. But that took years of therapy to understand.

And yet, I managed. I was obsessive and focused on doing things according to procedure, so I finished college with an A- average. I became the go-to person in the family for general information and trivia. Held jobs. Scheduled and kept meticulous 'To-Do' lists organized around my two-home arrangement. Doesn't that sound like someone who has it together? How could this someone have a mental illness? Sure, all of us get overwhelmed and stressed and overworked, but what made my situation a mental health disaster?

Why couldn't I continue on such a path for an indeterminate amount of time just fine, without a diagnosis, like others seemed to be able to?

I have asked myself that plenty of times. Life was hard enough, with parents divorced and my being moved between two countries, to ever want to slap a "mentally ill" label onto myself. Was it so that I could finally allow myself to experience the emotions I had buried? Maybe to feel like there was a real reason behind everything I had endured? Did the bliss of ignorance subside and make my illness undeniable, or was it something else?

I would like to think that meeting my now husband was the pivotal moment when I stopped being able to continue "just making it" and had to confront the reality of how truly unhappy I was. He cared for me, he spent time listening and didn't think any of my ideas were stupid, or any of my interests for that matter. He was forgiving when I wasn't my shining, smiling outward self.

Him showing me love opened up the floodgates for other emotions. I learned that plenty of people would be kind and caring. There was now no way to put two images of my life next to each other without seeing the earlier version crumble into pieces, filling me with disgust. I had a taste of joy and now I wanted it in my life all the time.

Taking The Road To Get Better, While Without Guarantees, Was What Would Create A Life Worth Living For Me.

Whether my lack of emotion was due to chemicals malfunctioning in my brain or circumstance was unimportant compared to the fact that I wanted to understand the truths about what my life really was like. What else had I believed to be okay within my environment and my feelings that truly wasn't?

I learned that it wasn't okay that my mother took me away from my home in the U.S. to Russia. That is called kidnapping. I learned that it was not right for my parents to expect my sister to raise me and take care of me while they were both alive, healthy, and earning more than decent income. I learned that not all families end in divorce. I learned that it was not ok for my uncle to slap my butt and tell me it would help it grow. It wasn't ok that I would vomit up my food to stay slim.

Are you overwhelmed yet hearing all of this at once? I was.

All of these were situations I had lived through, and they came rushing at me like a river. I became unable to see past them or shut them away any further. And that meant I wanted to them out. Whether by ending my life, taking medication, or going to therapy, I wanted them gone.

Since we can't run away from ourselves, I needed to learn tools to cope and come to terms with what how my life had been managed by others previously.

So now, you tell me. Was ignorance bliss or was awareness my savior? Was my diagnosis my crutch or my comfort and explanation?

Should you continue sleeping through the nightmare because you just want some rest, or should you violently wake yourself up and go through the painful process of dealing with things?

I am not sure whether feeling such relief is the case for every person who gets diagnosed with a mental illness, but I am here, aren't I? I am not suicidal (on more days than not). I partly own a home, I have a dog with a following on Instagram, I have bought myself a car, paid down half of my student loan, married the love of my life and been accepted into his family. I am now a writer and an advocate, an educator and presenter.

Did I live through all of that because I had no other options or did I learn about my illness and **choose** to recover because I needed attention? I don't think I had a choice either way.

Letter to Myself 10 Years Ago

DEAR SEVENTEEN-YEAR-OLD ME:

I am not going to ask how you are, because I know the answer is miserable and depressed. I know you have not used the word *depressed* confidently to describe how you're feeling, but I am happy to tell you that in the future, you will. You will also come to terms with the definitions of *Post-Traumatic Stress Disorder*[78], *Anxiety*[79] and the big one – "Antidepressants."[80] Weird, right?

You'll need to go through your journey to get there yourself, but I know you are holding onto a thread of hope that one day you will be okay. Okay is correct, but it won't come in the form you think *okay* means right now. You will not be cured, your depression is not temporary, but you do recover from those awful life-ending emotions you feel right now. It goes on and off, but ten years from now is a big year for you because of that journey.

On Writing
You mentioned before that you have a hard time letting yourself write. I implore you to keep at it, even if it's just short nonsense for yourself. It makes me so sad to think of all the time I did not write because I was afraid of my own judgment.

I know according to the laws of time travel I can't change the past, but I truly wish I could in this case. Yes,

---

[78] *https://www.nimh.nih.gov/health/topics/post-traumatic-stress-disorder-ptsd/index.shtml*
[79] *https://www.nimh.nih.gov/health/publications/generalized-anxiety-disorder-gad/index.shtml*
[80] *https://www.youtube.com/watch?v=o43RHZVdo5g*

you're an awesome yearbook editor, but I mean even keeping a diary, something to get you writing every day. I don't think that will change the course of things, but it may help you be a bit more prepared, with a sharper tool set for the day when writing becomes part of your job. No spoilers there either, I will let you wait until you're twenty-five to figure out what it is you need to do to bring yourself there.

It's Not Your Fault

Oh, how I wish I could hug you. In some ways, I do. Every day. Thanks to all those quotes I've seen, where I am supposed to remind my inner child that she's ok and taken care of. But I don't think you can feel those hugs through space-time, otherwise, you wouldn't need one. You deserve so much love, and it's really not your fault no one can give that to you presently.

Your family should be doing a better job truly raising you. They're less than half-assing it – they're blaming you for their own mistakes, making sure your self-esteem stays low so that you depend on them to bring you back up. I hope this helps confirm your suspicions, but I do understand that might take you another five years to truly believe me.

Dreams Do Come True

Reading back this letter, I realize I've focused on comforting you, because I wish I knew some of these things before.

Now. The good stuff. And there is so much! I want to address all the things you dream about when you lock yourself in the closet or the bathroom to cry. You achieve these things in the future, so, I will go through them one-by-one so that you hold on knowing that, yes, better things do lay ahead.

You know how dad often says "This is how this house runs, and once you grow up and earn your own money, you can call us, put us all on speaker and tell us to F***k off." I know you imagine this moment after a knife is thrown at you, or you are told to leave the house. It's often what motivates you to keep working and doing well. So that one day you can finally leave and never come back.

Well, it's not that dramatic, we still talk to dad, but you do leave! Really. It's been a few years since you cut ties with most of that family and I still look back at the moment when that all came to a head with pride. I don't want to ruin it for you, but it is as satisfying as you imagine it to be. I know you've resolved it will happen and that motivates you when things get especially tough. Keep at it.

Oh, Boy

Now, about the boy you've been pining over. I'll tell you what happens even though I know you won't listen to me anyway. He breaks your heart. Crushes it. Into small pieces.

A bunch of people are going to tell you "you're young, you'll be fine." Sure, that doesn't make it hurt less, but also know that the guy you've been dreaming of? You get to meet him in just another year and a half. And after you two grow together, you have the prettiest wedding ever. I know right now you think marriage is stupid, but can you imagine how amazing he is, that he makes you change your mind? Yeah, man! Totally worth the wait. You have an apartment and a dog. As I write this letter, our dog is on the blanket next to me, snuggled against my lap as I type. It's everything we've dreamed it would be, but better because it's real. And we wake up every morning grateful for it.

I know you asked me about our sister, well, she walks you down the aisle, so you can imagine how awesome that relationship will get. You'll re-connect with her, and it will be better than it ever was.

The Bitter-Sweet Part
Despite all of this you, unfortunately, still suffer from Depression. Because mental illness is a real thing and it doesn't care how awesome your life is. Right now, you're being told you're just "weak" and "clingy" and "stupid," but honestly, that's some crap. You have a chemical imbalance and that makes leaving dark thoughts rather difficult. In the future, you'll learn how to handle and manage them. Don't feel rushed (I am sure you will) or freak out (you will do that too) – you'll get there.

No reason to worry about this either: your illnesses do not define you, your other personality traits are way too big for that, but I think it will help you to know you can come to terms with it.

I know how much you beat yourself up, and just want to remind you that you are doing the best you can for the circumstances you are in. Truly, the odds are not in your favor and you are shining anyway. With the jobs you keep, the friendships you are fostering, and how well you do in school even though English is not your first language.

Oh wow, this ended up being so long. I hope you're not crying. I got a little teared up looking back but overall, I am proud of us.

And, by the way, crying does not make you "broken" or "whiney", I know you've heard all of those terms from others but you get even worse with using them towards yourself. If you keep telling yourself all of those awful things, of course, you're going to believe them. What's worse is that you will create cycles that you will continue to perpetuate for years.

Consider cutting yourself some slack. You're trying so hard, and if you continue working this hard, I promise you, you make it this far. And then we're going to keep working so that the next ten years will be worth writing about as well.

The community of incredible people you have surrounded yourself with now do work to make sure no one ever feels alone like you do now. The world gets brighter and vibrant once you embrace yourself.

    Keep inspiring me, kiddo. Thank you for everything you do that brings you here. I am so proud.

Love, *Mxiety*

What My Childhood Diary Taught Me About Having A Mental Illness

AFTER WRITING DOWN THE WORDS I wish I could tell myself ten years ago, I was inspired to go through my diary. I hadn't kept one consistently since I was twelve, and I regret that now. I stopped after one of my friends read it out loud and made fun of me for writing four pages mourning a dead bird I found on the boardwalk. I was mocked for being sensitive and stupid about dead animals[81] because clearly the only acceptable thing to write about is crushing on cute boys.

So, my dedication waned. I seldom wrote in a journal, if at all. When I did, all my notes were scattered and rarely properly dated. I kept more than one because so many notebooks were given to me as gifts and also as a safety precaution. There were scattered on various shelves, in closets, and drawers across my room. I figured the practice might confuse anyone who went in searching for written evidence of my hidden thoughts of which there were plenty because I was convinced that I was awful and not the circumstances I was in.

What I found as a result of my search was another dose of perspective, similar to that which came from writing the aforementioned letter. I don't know if handwriting is still a live form of journaling, I am sure all the cool kids keep theirs digitally. Writing, journaling, etc. offer a unique form of perspective that doctors have long confirmed to be incredibly helpful for mental health[82] because it keeps you letting things out, helps in organizing thoughts, and provides a place to put emotions which may not be welcome. Writing

---

[81] *https://mxiety.com/blog/calling-you-sensitive*
[82] *https://www.sciencedirect.com/science/article/pii/S0272735815000161*

is a powerful defense which took me about twenty years too long to pick up again.

Today, I regret that and hope to encourage others to never stop expressing themselves due to fear. I was afraid of my own thoughts and my own judgment as much as I was afraid of others', and I missed out on quite a bit of perspective. Thus, I implore you, don't let your mind stop you from putting words to a page.

Some of these might seem obvious. If they do to you, great! You are likely having a great time keeping a journal. Keep it up.

Venting Is Important
Growing up I was unable to vent my frustrations at home. When I did, I was either punished, told the situation was my fault, or completely ignored. When I look back it seems I only wrote in any of my journals if I was extremely upset. Sometimes, I even used it as a way to talk myself out of my suicidal thoughts. If you are a parent, reading this might be terrifying. A good parent would want to let their child know they are safe, especially if their thoughts betray them. But, I implore you to let your child have their privacy.

Thoughts we do not act upon, especially if we want to prevent acting upon them, deserve to be noted. It's part of the process that helps us move past and deal with traumatic situations. Writing helps you make sense of that jumble of thoughts like nothing else can. It is clear that I did not hurt myself, and I think writing was a vital part of that. As a child I thought about lots of weird stuff. I had lots of anxieties and fears which I could only express in writing without scaring anyone.

Reminders To Stay Resilient

It has also been extremely helpful for me to re-read what was written when I was in the moment, doubting myself and my own emotions. As a teen, I would sometimes flip back and see reminders, clear as day of how upsetting the situation I was in was due to repeated actions my family took. It had not been the first time a parent spoke to me that way, it helped me begin to consider that perhaps it was not my fault it was happening. Day to day in my home my judgment was constantly undermined and having written proof of similar emotions on previous occasions was crucial. The reminders helped keep my head level. They helped me remove myself from the cycle and remember to stay strong and trust my instincts: a quality people who are exposed to gaslighting[83] usually have a hard time comprehending well past the abuse being over.

In The Spirit Of Survival

Reading through my rationalizations then, I understand how far the human spirit will go to survive. I read how I forgave my family for the emotional pain I felt for all of those years. I had knives thrown at me, people making inappropriate comments, a parent who manipulated me instead of apologizing for their actions, and I got through it all. I am not completely without scars, but I am well and have created a wonderful life for myself in my adulthood.

As I read through the anguish, the poems, all of the words which at the time seemed silly to express, I can note clear timestamps of the progress I have made. Maybe not always as a writer, but certainly as someone recovering from a toxic parental relationship and Major Depression. I can see

---

[83] *https://www.psychologytoday.com/us/blog/here-there-and-everywhere/201701/11-warning-signs-gaslighting*

that spirit of survival in the hope that was ever present in those same poems and expressions of angst. More than anything, I wanted out of that nightmare with the notion that perhaps the future would be better. And it was.

I am grateful to young M for being resilient and continuing to work to ensure there was an end. I may not have been a perfect child, but at the very least I had the smarts to realize that perhaps my parents and I – even if the emotional abuse didn't count – likely didn't have personalities that meshed well. I am not entirely sure whether I had such perspective when I was younger, but I have certainly gained it now.

The most important point in all of this is that I wish I wrote more as a kid. I let someone steal my permission to create and then let that memory control my future. I certainly don't believe the world almost missed some brilliant writer or anything, I believe I missed out on learning self-value. I told myself writing was something to be done when someone is happy, when I was better. For a while, I couldn't write because it was too painful to access the scars of my past, writer's block in that sense was a defense mechanism. But there should be no gate that keeps us away from writing.

Once you are ready to find your voice, please don't let any thought in your mind stop you from letting your creativity flow. Fingers to a keyboard, pen to paper, whichever way you want to express yourself, don't let you stop you. From my experience, you'll be grateful you didn't.

Giving Myself Permission to Feel Better

"WHY IS IT," I asked myself first thing in the morning, "that I can't support my family by doing what I love?" To which my depressive brain, always ready with a snarky retort, would respond with something like "It must be because you're terrible. You're a failure and you should give up." An astute observer might note that this is a great example of All or Nothing Thinking[84]. I will note that it often runs my show. I start the gambit early and will likely repeat the call-response at least thirteen times a day.

What I have previously not admitted, is that I am honestly not sure what I would do without this voice in my head. Ideally, I would be more productive, but I can't help but think I would also feel as though I lost a friend.

First, please know that I am not sharing this to have someone to come and tell me that I am ok and am kind and worthy. I've done enough years of therapy to know that those kinds of affirmations need to be learned firsthand, without needing to rely on others to confirm them.

I am sharing because I am sure many out there have similar thoughts and I want them to know they are not alone. If you are not one of those people, I want to emphasize how cyclical and self-fulling such thoughts are, so that you understand why it's not possible to just stop them.

Having depression, experiencing these and many other symptoms every minute you are awake means you can't just be cheered up. You can't take a walk and feel better. You'll just be a depressed person on a walk. That being said…

I have had therapists remind me that unless I *wanted* progress, nothing about my condition would ever change.

---

[84] *https://psychcentral.com/blog/5-ways-to-expand-all-or-nothing-thinking/*

Well, I certainly didn't want to continue feeling endless despair and see nothing but darkness ahead, so I felt taken aback. "You think I want this? Who's the one who needs therapy here?" I would fume as the thoughts filled my mind. But then again, why was it just seemed like no matter the work I did, Depression persisted[85].

If I am completely honest, I kind of thought that once I had gathered the courage to talk about my feelings with a stranger that would be all I needed. That was the work. Sitting across the room from a therapist and reliving my nightmares was not easy. How could it that not be enough?

After all, the analogy works for most other doctors. When I have sinus issues, I see my doctor, take a decongestant, maybe an antibiotic, and call it a day. The nose doesn't have a say in not being congested, and the problem diminishes. Our minds are a bit more complex, however, and don't work quite the same.

Turns out, there's a difference between getting yourself to a place where you start the process, going through the assigned steps, and then actually healing. Sorry, what I truly mean is giving yourself *permission* to actually heal.

Simply put, I may have wanted to stop being depressed, but I did not think I *deserved* to feel well. Only good people feel well. I would remind myself that since "people like me are a waste of space, I can only get to a certain point before I have to and think of my true worth –nothing." Dark stuff, right? As a bonus, the self-accusation is purposefully vague enough that there is no blocking it with logic or outside kindness.

Making good active choices, such as going to the doctor, taking a yoga class, taking medication daily without missing a dose are all part of getting better, but they only

---

[85] *https://www.apa.org/topics/depression/index*

uncovered the surface of my tangled mind. Just like you can go to the gym and kind of move weights up and down, you can go to a therapist and just talk. You might even cry, but none of that compares to actually teaching yourself to be happy when you don't even understand what true joy might be.

Let me back up and explain the level of self-doubt that helped this prevail.

I would start feeling down. My husband would come into the room and ask if I would like to play video games or hang out with him, but I would decline, saying that I was not feeling well. While I wasn't lying, there was another layer. When I was sad, I unquestionably also believed that I didn't deserve to do anything I enjoyed until the feeling had passed and I truly *earned* the right to feel better. As if feeling happiness is a reward and not something all humans are entitled to experience.

I would go to the therapist and listen to what she had to say. We would talk about catching my negative self-talk and replacing it with positive affirmations. Then I would leave the office and immediately think about how weak I was for needing to see a therapist at all. Even if I did catch myself thinking these awful things, since they were my default for so long, I felt like I was powerless to change them. "My mind just works against me," I would rationalize. Or worse yet, "this is who I am." This meaning, a *Depressed Person*, not a *Person with Depression*.

Now here is the moment, you, the reader, might be expecting I learned all about changing my thinking to be more positive and finally had a breakthrough.

That's not what happened. I couldn't convince myself that I was okay overnight, after spending over twenty-five years of my life telling myself I wasn't. All I have been able to do as of recently is just *consider* that it might be ok for me to not focus on the soul-crushing darkness that consumes my every thought. That is a small, yet broad step to truly feeling better.

I began considering that "What if I wasn't the undeserving sh*t that I have been thinking I am? What then? What qualities do I have?" Well, it turns out, thinking I am *not* undeserving set off an avalanche of many more positive *what-ifs*. If I am not garbage, maybe I also deserve to be loved (just like everybody else does).

AGREEING WITH SMITHS "HOW SOON IS NOW"
Could it be true that my friends actually do want to be around me? Could it be that I am not a failure? Spending so much time convincing myself that I was horrible sure created a huge list of things to reverse and reconsider. Until, finally, I thought, "perhaps having a bad day does not make me a bad person."

Two things helped me get out of this cycle:
1. Leaping over[86] the awful feeling by faking a belief that I am not horrible
2. Admitting that for me, it was important to stay on medication[87]

The medication helped adjust the chemicals in my mind that kept me dependent on awful thoughts, while pretending to like myself made me start treating myself with some kindness. The combination of both is what sustains my positive emotions on my good days now.

---

[86] *https://www.mxiety.com/blog/steps-to-finally-take-the-leap*
[87] *https://mxiety.com/blog/feeling-better-needing-medication*

I needed permission to be hopeful that my life would not always be run by depression. Permission I would not grant myself in case I was wrong, so as to avoid the pain of failing. On many days, the painful thoughts of being undeserving still creep in. That is very likely to keep happening for the rest of my life.[88] However, the mere assumption that I am not complete garbage is what will keep those days further apart. It will let me look forward to the days when I do feel well, because I now I suspect I deserve them too.

88

https://www.ncbi.nlm.nih.gov/pmc/articles/PMC2648513/?ref=driverlayer.com/web

What They're Really Saying When They Call You 'Sensitive'

BEING BILINGUAL, WHILE BENEFICIAL in many ways, can sometimes make it harder to understand subtext. It's no secret that some words can be maliciously used to hit you right in the heart. To those who are working through their understanding of the world and feel at odds with how they are feeling versus what they are told they *should* be feeling – this story is for you.

I have always been a bubbly, excitable human. I loved singing and dancing in front of family because it made them smile and laugh. However, I was also labeled as *sensitive*. *Sensitive*, a word which when spoken by my parents had many meanings, but none of them kind or caring. Most often it bore the connotation of one who is too easily upset. And since the word faulted me for reacting in such a manner, no matter what happened, they were absolved of entertaining the possibility their wrong-doing could have been responsible for my feeling such an emotion.

But this happened when I was a child, with too many things which were too out of my control for anyone to place rightful blame on me. Could I have been a sensitive kid? Sure, but that label does not absolve anyone of the responsibility of being empathetic.

I missed my mom and got upset when she left me in a foreign country without saying goodbye, I cried a lot as a result– *sensitive*. I watched Jurassic Park with my mother when I was six and was scared —*sensitive*. After all, if I wasn't sensitive, my mother would have stayed away for another year so that she could accomplish her goals, and she wouldn't have to leave the theatre after paying $6 to see the movie (1997).

As a result, I was growing up with the clear-as-mud message: If you can't tough it out and if someone has to take care of you, you will be an unlovable nuisance.

In reality, this made me about as tough as a soft-boiled egg: a seemingly hard shell that could crack at the slightest pressure, revealing a soft, dribbling mess on the inside. I came off strong, overly excitable, and "I don't care if you think I am nuts, because I am definitely nuts and you outta know it" became my long winded, but accurate motto.

I was desperate to be liked, so I smiled and acted like a clown, but should you poke at the fact that this was a charade, I quickly crumbled, usually crying and thinking about how I would have enjoyed having the ability to disappear completely. Thus, as an adolescent, *sensitive* meant: easily offended by the slightest comment.

As a young adult, I stopped being able to pretend I was happy and lovable, because I didn't feel it at all. The traumatic childhood events and faulty chemical brain structure came together to definitively throw me into a state of depression.[89] It couldn't be called *depression*, since such a term would never be acknowledged by my family with anything but purposeful ignorance (meaning: if you ignore it, it's not a problem).

I would have days where getting out of bed was incredibly difficult, days I was just mad for no reason, followed by days when anything could set me off crying and finally days where I felt nothing at all. Thus, *sensitive* started to mean: someone who can't pull themselves together.

The final context for the word came to me after an event at my grandma's house in Brooklyn. She was showing me something, trinkets and the like when she pulled out a photograph. She was in the middle of explaining that it was one of the few pictures she had of me as a child in Russia

---

[89] *https://mxiety.com/blog?category=The%20Origins*

when I burst into tears. *Burst* being used quite literally in this context. At first, I felt warmth and joy from the memory but that was quickly overcome with sadness. I remembered when the picture was taken, the wallpaper, the dishes on the table, the smell of old candle wax as it burned, the hum of the old television set. It was New Year's Eve 1998 in Russia. I have asked (several therapists) and being flooded by emotions from an image is completely normal, being so overwhelmed with sensory recall from the event that you start to hysterically cry and become inconsolable—isn't.

If this reaction was a single occurrence, my family would have been more than justified to have brushed this off by explaining my *sensitivity* to grandma. Teenagers are moody and dramatic, no doubt about it.

This was about the moment that I realized something must not have been correct. I had been mentioning I was not feeling well, and it was starting to feel like the employment of *sensitive* was a deliberate gesture to further dismiss the notion that I may have been unwell. All of the connotations used to that point came crashing through my mind.

Could *sensitive* have meant: attention-seeking? I couldn't even control myself enough to act in such a way to try to get attention if I wanted to. It seemed concerning that no one wanted to help me act normal since my *sensitivity* had clearly passed regular levels. Think about yourself now, should someone in front of you burst into tears, would you react with empathy or would you walk by? Maybe I am wrong to place such a dilemma out there, but I should hope you would act on the latter.

This post is a very long way of saying: before you blame yourself or call yourself *stupid*, *weak*, or *sensitive*, no matter your current mental health state, consider what these words truly mean. It helps to think about how you came to associate these terms with yourself—was it completely your own doing, or were there enough repeated encounters with people using language as a tool to make themselves feel better about their actions?

Consider what those people were saying about their feelings towards you. How much effort they put into repeating one word, with the specific purpose of promoting their particular inflection onto it. "That's a stupid thing to do," here meaning something occurred without being given much thought. Compared to, "**You** were so stupid to do that," meaning you did something thoughtlessly in malice which affected the person you were speaking with.

Here is the official definition of *Sensitive* from Merriam-Webster.[90] You may note that most of the definitions are correct for the situations I described, in which case a connotation was created to insinuate negative meaning. At other times, the word was used completely out of context to help absolve accountability.

I spent too many years blaming myself for other's mistakes. I hope I can cut down that time for you.

Definition of sensitive:
1: sensory sense
        a: receptive to sense impressions
        b: capable of being stimulated or excited by external agents (such as light, gravity, or contact)
2: highly responsive or susceptible: such as
        a (1): easily hurt or damaged; especially : easily hurt emotionally

---

[90] *https://www.merriam-webster.com/dictionary/sensitive*

(2): delicately aware of the attitudes and feelings of others
b: excessively or abnormally susceptible : hypersensitive
c: readily fluctuating in price or demand
d: capable of indicating minute differences : delicate
e: readily affected or changed by various agents (such as light or mechanical shock)
f: highly radiosensitive
3: concerned with highly classified government information or involving discretionary authority over important policy matters
b: calling for tact, care, or caution in treatment: touchy
4: having or showing concern for a specified matter — usually used in combination

Why You Should Be Your Own Friend

ONE DAY I WAS BERATING MYSELF in my therapist's office when she asked if I thought I was a good friend.

"I'm sure I let people down sometimes, but I try to be caring, compassionate and non-judgmental," I said, barely hiding my *what are you getting at* face.

"Do you often tell your friends they're stupid?"

"Ha, No. I always make sure they know how amazing I think they are."

"Do you tell them you don't have time to deal with their problems, that they should push them away and handle them later?"

"I...no. Wait a minute. That's different. I need to push things away so that I can be a better, kinder, more attentive. And I am not smart enough, if I was I wouldn't be depressed."

(Seriously this how I think of myself when I am at a low point).

"Do you think being mean to your friends helps them become better, kinder people?"

Now, I'm sure you've pieced together her message with me.

Those of us who want to be good friends try to be kind, caring, and encouraging. We know no one wants to be friends with someone who calls them stupid or dismisses their problems, so we work hard to be good and never bully others. But it seems they often don't mind being bullies to themselves.

And that's exactly how self-loathing grows.

Who enjoys spending time with someone who offers hatred and bitterness when it's so much more pleasant to be encouraged, loved and supported? Moreover, if someone were to treat your loved one so poorly, wouldn't you advise them to stand up for themselves? Remind them that they deserve more respect?

Understanding this is how I have come to realize I need to work harder on becoming my own friend. I was tired of dreading my own mind. I wanted to be happier and able to enjoy being alone. I have found that working on becoming my own friend has helped me in many ways.

To Be Less Nervous About Spending Time Alone
There are many other human complexities that make it difficult to spend time alone. Countless studies have been done on the importance[91] of feeling like part of a community.[92] Slowly, I have learned that it's not just the isolation that used to make me hate being by myself. It was because silence offered a playground for my meanest thoughts to surface, which also meant it rendered me extremely unproductive. Since I love writing, and I need silence or something near it to be able to focus, I was determined to learn.

"So," I thought, "how would I encourage a friend to write?" Well, I would tell them how much I enjoy reading things they create, how impactful their words can be to read, how dedicated they must be able to complete something like that.

Then I made a deal with myself: if when I am alone I could think of five nice things about my writing, I would have to lift the metaphorical block I kept hitting and let myself put something down on paper (or screen).

Yes, exactly like a bribe. It worked. It still works. Not totally foolproof, but it works more times than it doesn't. I gave myself permission to accept that I wasn't the worst

---

[91] *https://econtent.hogrefe.com/doi/10.1024/1421-0185/a000186*
[92] *https://econtent.hogrefe.com/doi/10.1027/0227-5910/a000356*

writer in the history of time, and therefore my attempts to write were valid. Eventually, I started associating being alone with being productive and started enjoying that prospect altogether.

To Feel More Confident About Finding New Friends / Partners
Being desperate and as afraid as possible are not the ideal qualities we look for in a mate.[93] Unfortunately, I had incredibly low self-esteem in my teens. Since I didn't think I had value to others, I constantly said negative things and put myself down during interactions. I negged myself so often that I created a cycle.

But who should ever be nice to someone who acts like that? Should've been Me! Once I started to break the cycle and stopped starting every interaction by being unkind to myself, I felt more confident that I deserved nicer treatment from others. I would stop looking for people to reinforce everything I hated about myself, and would instead find kinder people. They would be kinder friends, and I would not want to be alone to protect my feelings.

Once a positive loop was reinforced and repeated a few times, I started feeling better and became much more approachable in general. That created more social encounters which made it more likely to make lovely friends.

The hardest part about this one, is that it took me some time to learn how *what* I liked about myself. What nice things could I say about myself without cringing or feeling pretentious (or arrogant)? What was I willing to admit I liked about myself? Once I knew what that was, it became easier to make a case for someone else to love me.

---

[93] *https://www.psychologytoday.com/us/blog/maybe-its-just-me/201310/does-everyone-find-confidence-attractive*

To Start Being One's Own Cheerleader

Teachers are very likely to understand this one without an example, but for the rest of us...have you talked to a friend who was feeling low and found that your joke lifted their spirits? Or someone who really enjoys cooking / drumming / playing basketball / dancing but was convinced they were no good at it? Now, what did better to keep that person perfecting their craft: telling them to quit? That they're not trying hard enough? Or offering help and encouragement?

Same works for every one of us on an internal level. If I kept telling myself I could never write and that there is no sense in trying, I would keep believing exactly that.

Recently-and this was much harder than it sounds-I tried encouraging myself the way I would my loved ones. When I heard myself about to say, "I don't know anything, everything I write comes out stupid," I caught the bubbling thought and would push myself to think instead: "I really enjoy researching mental health topics, maybe I can *try* to write about that."

I replaced "I might as well not even try writing, since I can't even finish one article," with "I've been thinking about this other thing a lot, I might as well just jot it down."

I don't do this enough, but when I do, it always works and gets me to be more productive. Clinical Depression is no joke and it's very difficult to motivate yourself when there is a chemical imbalance as the root cause for such negative emotions to begin with, but it doesn't hurt to try. What does hurt relentlessly is to continue the cycle of self-abuse unchecked.

The key to moving towards all of these initiatives was the one small notion that maybe I could start working with myself instead of against. Maybe I could become my own friend, so that I could be there for myself when no one was around and could provide me with all the exact words I needed.

If you're alone, get comfortable hanging out with you. Show yourself that you appreciate your own company and that you do not take all of your hard work to be a good person for granted. Act like you're friends with yourself. Watch a Disney movie together. And if you hear your friend think they are stupid, list out loud all the wonderful things they *actually* are. And it wouldn't hurt to say "I love you," either. Just to bring the point home.

Mistakes I Have Made While Trying To Help Friends Who Needed Me

Disclaimer: names and situations have been adjusted to protect identities and due to memory faults.

As much as it pains me to admit, I've made a lot of mistakes when it comes to helping my friends with mental illnesses. I deeply regret the friendships I have lost, when I reacted or behaved in a way that was what the person requesting was expecting or needed at the time.

Returning readers know I promote the motto "be the light." The caveat of this, just like with the motto "treat others the way you want to be treated," is that not everyone wants the same type of treatment from each other. i.e. "I expected this kind of light/support from you and what you did instead was inexcusable"—with the caveat that everyone has their own version of inexcusable. The result is separation due to irreconcilable differences. I use that specific term because, yes, good, close friendships feel like marriages; when they fall apart a huge part of yourself can be lost, just as it would be in a divorce.

A few scenarios come to mind that I feel might help mental illness allies avoid mistakes. My hope is that through my attempt to share these objectively, someone reading can draw conclusions about actions to take in the future and which to avoid.

Here is how I have unfortunately mishandled some situations.

The Friend Who Threatens Suicide
A few years ago, I was sitting in a hotel room, a few states away from home. It was scary and painful to read the text message: "I don't want to live anymore. I haven't eat'n in

hours. I'm going to leave my house and walk until I pass out." I tried to call. No one picked up. If I was closer, I would have driven over and talked to this person face-to-face. But I was three states away. Due to this person's ongoing battle with depression, they were not included in the group of people who went away, by their own request. Since Major Depressive Disorder plays well with suicidal thoughts, it didn't take long for our friend to start feeling worse and even seemingly abandoned.

In panic, I followed the rules I had learned in therapy. If someone might be a harm to themselves or others, police should be called to protect their life.[94] So, I called the police in our hometown to request a civilian check. Our friend was home and okay, but I maintain that suicidal threats should always be taken seriously as they are usually a final attempt at getting the attention and help one needs. I would rather be the person who was ostracized for calling the police than the naïve one, whose friend died. I maintain this stance.

The Person Who Has Too Much Going On To Help
A few years back, I was the one on the phone crying. I was home alone and the scary, invasive suicidal thoughts were creeping in again. I knew I would never act on them, but sobbing and blubbering on the phone, I am sure the friend on the other side of the line was at a loss for words. I just kept repeating, "please stay on the line, I don't want to be alone, I am scared." The friend had to get off the phone. I didn't blame him/her, but when I asked about it a few days later, the explanation for not staying on the call was "well how was I supposed to know what to do, you sounded bad. I am not feeling well either, so I am not sure how I can keep helping you."

---

[94] *https://www.mayoclinic.org/diseases-conditions/suicide/in-depth/suicide/art-20044707*

Since then, I have found the support I was looking for then, but within a new group of friends. It's amazing how just being there and listening helps every time. I even have a friend now who follows the philosophy of "hey we're both stuck, why don't we try to support each other through it?[95]" I think the reason my old friend was scared, was because they may have felt responsible once they knew they couldn't do enough. The more I needed them, the more they ended up pushing me away. I was likely not a very good support buddy at the time either, but I am grateful we both tried in our own ways. Even if it wasn't enough for either of us.

The Friend Who Won't Admit To Needing Help
A couple of months back, I was reading a wall of text appearing so rapidly in an online chat that I was scrolling frantically to keep up. It was the desperate typing of someone who had lost friends over how their mental illness had made them behave. The strings were so many words, all berating one person or another for "not being there" and being "selfish and narcissistic." The only response I had was not appreciated. "I think you should talk to a professional. I don't think I can help untangle this for you, the way a professional will." Of course, in that instant, I also became "unsupportive" and "another person to let me down."

Since then, this friend has reached out to me on and off. Although they were verbally abusive when I reminded them that a professional would be the best way to get back to a normal, fulfilling life, without suicidal thoughts and so much anger, I stay in touch. Hoping that once they get the help they need, they'll understand where I came from. I wish

---

[95]

http://static1.1.sqspcdn.com/static/f/1542080/27739393/1509938306177/comi ccrushed.jpg?token=DOt%2Ba2veT2Fkh73RqrDv1%2BekODY%3D

that I was qualified to provide psychological assistance, but I know I am not.

Looking back, I hope all of these people remember that they are not alone.

In all these situations I was the person who could not help, when help was needed. But I have been suicidal and have had the police take me to the hospital—and I was grateful for that. I have stayed on the line for someone who felt scared and alone even though I had something else I needed to do. I was the person who lost many friends before I accepted professional help. Of course, all of these experiences have shaped how I react. They've all taught me something.

It's all a matter of how an individual perceives support. If you are suffering, I hope you have found the support system that works best for you. If you know someone who is suffering, try to breach the topic of how they wish for you to handle certain scenarios, so that you are prepared and know which actions will be best.

Am I Afraid Of The Dark?

I DON'T KNOW WHAT I'M AFRAID OF more: darkness, loneliness, or the silence they both can bring with them. Once the lights go off, my brain churns in overtime. The shadows shift into something that isn't there, and all my biggest fears seem to be real. For me, the dark is the time for each memory to play out anew.

Age 6: Due to my parents' relationship being on the rocks, my dad slept in our finished basement. Like any basement to a child, it seemed dark and scary anytime I opened the door and looked down the stairs. While my dad slept there, that darkness seemed harmless and warm. One day I ran down only to see the bed was neatly made, and it had apparently been made for several days. Later that day my mom confirmed that he wasn't coming home. My dad decided to leave and start a new family. After that, anytime I would approach the top step, I would freeze up and turn around.

Age 7: One spring day, my mother picked up my belongings and without telling me that the move would be permanent, relocated me to Russia. She left there a week after introducing me to the rowdy Greek family I apparently belonged to but had only seen once otherwise. They were kind and welcoming, but they were all strangers. Because she "didn't want me to get upset" she didn't even say "goodbye", so I didn't learn that I was left to live with this new family for two days. I recall that most nights I lay in my couch-turned-bed, starring at the stucco ceiling, wondering what I did to make her leave. I would fall asleep after crying a lot, promising to myself that I would be good if she ever came back. She did, three months later. I didn't leave her side for two weeks, which is how I earned the nickname *prelipuchka* (sticker).

Age 15: Sleep was an elusive concept. I would spend my nights staring at the glow-in-the-dark butterflies stuck to my ceiling. Eventually, I removed them as my imagination was getting so creative, that they started to morph into horrible shapes in front of my eyes. My mind would keep reeling, so my body refused to rest no matter how tired I was. After a while, I was afraid of my bed, so I would lay on the floor with blankets. This just became part of a new routine: go to bed, read, watch TV, put my bedding on the floor and on a few lucky nights, get some rest.

All of the above is the reason darkness feels so loaded with emotions. I associate it with feeling small, unwanted and isolated. Like I am six or seven again and incapable of doing anything to help myself if left alone.

Of course, the older I got, the less likely there would be people surrounding me and the worse my sleeping patterns got. Through my first year in college, I would wake up in a cold sweat. I had a recurring dream that I was only sleeping in my dorm because I had been kicked out of my home. It didn't help that when everyone moved in their parents were always there, exchanging saying tearful goodbyes after unpacking cars with stuff carefully selected to make the dorm a home. Every semester, as my boyfriend helped bring my things up to my room, I would stop midway to stare at the families. If they looked, I pretended to adjust whatever I was holding before moving along.

It took time to gather enough not-threatening experiences that I actually, sometimes, kind of, maybe enjoy spending time quietly. Even so, if I know I am going to be alone for an extended period of time, I do things to prepare myself for it. For example, my friends note that I love being a host. A small part of that, is so that I can create moments to recharge with. This way, when my mind offers me my worst fears, I can evoke noisy, happy memories to counter them.

I have other ways to try to desensitize myself daily. I force myself to sit in silence when I eat if my husband's late at work. When I sit down to write, I give myself a moment after turning everything off just feel the lack of sound inside my eardrums for as long as I can.

Writing is actually the biggest inconvenience for this phobia. Since, unfortunately, I don't write well unless I am surrounded by silence. Darkness comes with silence, so I am working to re-associate the silence with the joy of self-expression it permits; giving it another purpose other than letting all my worst fears run wild in my mind. One thing that helped with this phobia was getting a dog. My pup not only makes for great company, but also requires consistent belly rubs, so I am assured he'll at least stick around for those.

At 27, I am just now truly learning to dive into silence instead of trying to jump over it. I try to take it as an opportunity to clear my mind, and handle my fears so that they do not come in the middle of the night. I welcome it, compared to the chaos of the rest of the world...though this doesn't work every time.

In fact, as I write this, I am crying over the irrational fear my husband will never come back and that my friends left not because they had to go home, but because they hate me. This considering I literally have my dog on my lap and my phone on the stand beside me with my friends' messages, asking when they should come over next.

Anxiety isn't rational, though its main claim to fame is being able to convince you that it is. As I approach this piece to edit, I've purposefully turned off all the lights, turned on a crackling wood-wick candle, sat back with my laptop and tea, and the only thought that crosses my mind is: "bring it".

How to Finally 'Take The Leap' In Three Steps

IN THE WEEK PRECEDING IT, through the month after New Year's Day I hear the question, *what's your resolution?* a lot. Instead of rambling on how putting that kind of pressure onto yourself is only going to make one less likely to follow through, I ask us to simply refocus our attention onto goals instead of resolutions.

For probably about five years, my resolution was to smile more, because I was afraid I would disappoint myself with anything more involved. I am a bubbly person, so I smile even if I am depressed. Easy Peasy! But last year I gave myself permission to set a goal (yes that means one I might fail). Without a specific timeframe in mind, I felt a decreased pressure to live up to a very strict, high standard I hold my ideas up to in my mind. Finally, I was permitted to think of creating something to help others feel less alone (like I had) while suffering from mental illness. That something became Mxiety.

Step zero: relieve the pressure
My depression monster has always said horrible things inside my mind, which often effects the things I give myself permission to do. Most often, I do not let myself even consider that I can make anything that isn't a waste of time for the reader. To let myself off the hook, I set a small goal: to write something, anything. Whatever I wrote, I could then use to help me dive further into what I might want to create.

A poem. Two words. A sentence. Something that I would not proof-read, but just type onto the screen. I was still so scared. So unforgiving, even with such a small goal. I took a leap above my thoughts and wrote. It ended up being over 200 words.

Step one: start somewhere
For the next year and change, I would use this method to talk myself into writing. I was already fortunate enough to have an amazing editor in an incredible friend. I knew he could sense when I hadn't proof-read, but he always believed that I could make something decent, so he patiently advised and offered revisions. I didn't always go back to follow through with re-writes but I finally saw value to my thoughts. Overall, because the thoughts were out of my mind and onto a page, I started considering them more and being more patient with their evolution as I edited the pieces I found worthy. Those pieces had some idea in common, but I was not sure what it was.

Step one and a half: get obsessed with an idea that feels bigger than your personal comfort
I have lived with mental illness for as long as I can consciously remember. When depression would come around with awful ideas, I would wonder what all of this suffering was for. I didn't give into the horrible thoughts, but felt like that had to be for a reason. I was hanging around, barely living with all this head noise, I needed a purpose to keep going.

    I decided that one day I would do something to help people like me. I didn't know how, but I promised I would keep coming back to this idea. Depression is worth having if I can help others get through it. Bizarre, yes? But there is it is.

Step two: find someone who believes in you + step one

One day, I jolted out of bed. I could never write without a pseudonym if I dared to post my writing publicly, which I desperately wanted to do to reach out to others who may have felt like me.

Mxiety was the name that woke me up. I sheepishly laughed off the notion as I explained my idea to my husband. I had been mulling it over, but now I had said it out loud. He loved it. "Let's grab the domain and user names," he suggested. I was worried it was a stupid waste of money, just like other things I had started, but he was determined. "I'd be willing to be out $10 if this isn't an investment," he explained while entering our credit card number.

Step Three: steps one and two combined, repeatedly
After doing lots of research (aka being scared and finding reasons why I should stop during every step of the way) I started an Instagram page—a leap. I started a free trail for a website host—another leap. I worked on the website—another leap. I paid for a full year of hosting and the site became public—another leap. I showed it to my friends—another leap. I kept writing—holy crap, I am doing this—leap. I showed it to more friends and made a Facebook group—leap. I started a Twitch stream, which I then edited into a YouTube video-Huge Leap!

I kept being afraid and jumping to try the thing I wanted to do anyway. It's not about "faking it" but rather acknowledging the fear and doing something anyway. You know you're going to be afraid no matter what, might as well try something new while you're busy being anxious.

Before I broke up my goals, I was facing a roaring river, attempting to run across without drowning or getting hurt. With each goal, it was as if I set a stone. Once I jumped onto that stone, I placed another one before stepping forward. And so on, until I was on a path, with so much determination, that there was no way I was returning to the same shore. Even if I am not sure what is on the other side, I knew I wanted to start moving towards it.

I am well into the river at this point. I am still freaking out. Every night before a broadcast, I panic. Who am I to talk on such a sensitive subject? Who cares what I think? What makes me special? But more than anything, I just want to keep going. I am so grateful that I have this much support to keep leaping across.

I broke my resolution into smaller goals without deadlines. And with that, got ahead of my mind, leaping faster than my negative thoughts could catch up. I hope you find the courage to start the journey across your river. And if needed, I hope I can offer a steady hand to you as we go.

A Letter to My Depression

DEAR DEPRESSION,

You won last night. I was so upset with myself and you that spent the night in bed, crying on and off. I would say *I hope you're happy*, but of course, I already know you're not. And even though you left in a huff, satisfied with how you escalated things, I know you'll be back.

This morning I got the fight back in me and I'm mad about how you behaved[96]. It seems silly to be communicating like this, but I wanted to get this letter out to you before you came back, so that you know where we stand going forward.

Let's review your points, shall we? What is it you said? Oh. That I am a piece of garbage. That I don't deserve to be loved and all my friends will leave me eventually. That I can't do anything right and should just give up trying. Is that right? What proof do you have?!

Those are some crazy, grandiose statements. They are based on nothing. I mean, I would never say something hurtful like that to anyone I know, but apparently, you can say that to me all the time. Well, it's not ok. It's hurtful and gets me super upset; especially since you like to repeat yourself over and over until I am (or at the very least, close to) having a full-on panic attack.

Let's, just for a second, assume that you are right. Where do we go from there? Sure, maybe before this year I didn't have friends who understood what it's like to have to drag you around. And yes, even my relatives thought I made you up since I am "just so sensitive". But that's exactly the

---

[96] *https://mxiety.com/blog/how-i-admit-to-having-mental-illness*

reason I found good friends and stopped talking to those relatives—because I learned how full of lies you are.

I know this is your way of egging me on, hoping that I will do something really drastic. Maybe even hurt myself in some way. But nope, I won't do that.

Thankfully, I have learned that there are kind people out there, who will listen and help however they can. They are friends and doctors and even strangers who work hard to make sure I don't take your words to heart and do anything drastic.

And don't you DARE go to someone else and try to pull the same crap on them. Because if I am around, so help me, I will fill the room with so much love and joy, you won't know what hit you.

You go low and I'll go high (thanks Michelle for the tip), if not higher.

We're stuck together for the foreseeable future. I can't imagine we will ever get along since I would rather not have you in my life, but we will definitely need to co-exist. If I could, believe me, I wouldn't hesitate to stop all communication with you.

Unfortunately, since you reside in my head, due to my lack of serotonin, I can't. I'm using medication now to make up for the chemical imbalance and seeing a therapist to learn better behaviors. Hopefully, that'll help me prepare, so that the next time you show up, I won't be so caught off guard with your declarations.

Oh, and one more thing. Dinner's at 7. Please come on time **and** with an appetite. Those meals are prepared with love and care and I can't let you keep ruining them by making everything taste bland.

Sincerely,
Mxiety

Why I Continue Fighting Having Mental Illness

I GO ON CAMERA WITH MY FRIENDS and promote getting professional help. I talk about going to the doctor, being diagnosed and admitting to having a problem as the first steps towards feeling better. I hope that my stories offer some kind of help.

Because of the stigma, getting help for mental illnesses is not easy, which is why I also try to practice what I preach. I go to a therapist. I take medication.

I also would be lying if I said I was okay with being sick. I go through spurts of being exceedingly angry with myself. Mad at my brain. My body. My genetics. But mostly, I am mad at the disease.

When I am in the right state of mind and not being eaten alive by depression—bedridden and crying all day—I am upset because of all of the time I have wasted bedridden and crying. To have something take away my ability to spend time with friends, enjoy foods I love, with very little control to stop it—it's just not a fair.

Of the seven stages of acceptance[97] (in grieving the loss is of my mind) I am stuck in **Anger**. And I don't think I should move from it. You see, being angry at this disease is what keeps me seeing a psychiatrist.[98] It's what keeps me going to counseling sessions.

---

[97] *https://psychcentral.com/lib/the-5-stages-of-loss-and-grief/*
[98] *https://www.psychiatry.org/patients-families/what-is-psychiatry*

I Am So Mad, That It Makes Me Want To Fight. I Want To Punch Depression Right In Its Shadowy Face. I Want To Kick Anxiety. I Want To Rip Through Every Flashback PTSD Brings.

Unfortunately, that means I have the mentality that these things *can be beaten*, whereas research says that someone diagnosed with mental illnesses will likely have to fight more than once. Sure, you can beat the main symptoms, in fact that's why you get into the ring.[99] However, it's realizing you're in a ring in the first place, that gives you a fair chance at a long, fulfilling life while continuing to fight.[100]

Sometimes I go down because, after swinging for months, I get exhausted. Am I still mad? Yes. Upset? You bet. But the fight is so unfair, I slip up and I let depression's left hook hit me right in the gut. And once a mental illness gets one good punch in, it can keep hitting until you go down for a long time.

At the end of that fight, I know I fought well, using all the techniques my coach (therapist) trained me to do. I might fall, but I know that I did the best I could. It's almost as though I am going down on my own terms. I know that I need to give in for a bit, but it is so that I can keep going in the long run.

On The Other Hand, It Feels Way Worse When I Go Down Because I Got Too Proud To Admit My Ongoing Problem

---

[99] *https://lifehacker.com/the-misconceptions-about-mental-illness-we-need-to-unle-1711647132*
[100] *https://themighty.com/2016/03/medication-doesnt-cure-mental-illness/*

I don't need to fight, I tell myself, *I'm too good to be someone forced to live in the ring.* And I am so wrong then, it's not even funny.

Like insulin to a diabetic, SSRIs keep my neurotransmitters working the way they were meant to. I wouldn't kick a crutch from under someone with a broken leg, but I seem to not mind opening my own carefully sutured scar and watching myself bleed out. I take myself off of the meds that have helped me and sometimes even skip a few behavioral sessions.

Being mad and being proud are the opposite sides of the same coin. The difference is, being mad equips me to keep fighting. Being proud will not stop the negative thoughts and panic attacks, it's just another reason I stop fighting. Pride makes me think I am too good to have to battle at all so when the fight comes to me, I am unprepared.

Don't be proud, stay in the ring. At least, as long as I am here, mad and still fighting. This way, mental illness is less likely to catch us by surprise. Let us admit that we need to fight, even though it hurts that it's more than others have to.

Whether you're mad, or just **over** not feeling 100%, please stay in the ring with me. Because if I know that other people are in the ring with me, if I know that they've fought the same demons and came out stronger in the long run, there is no exhaustion that will keep me from wanting to provide an assist when mental illness decides to hit while you're not looking. In the ring, I will have your back.

What It Costs To Have Anxiety

MOST PEOPLE CAN NEVER TRULY understand the currency of anxiety. Each letter typed is worth about 3 negative thoughts. Now before you get worried about the negative-thought-to-word conversion rate, perhaps wait for me to lay it out below. And if you're that concerned, maybe it's because you would like to know what the conversation will leave you with in your own struggle?

Here's the going rate:

Having to make a decision will place you into insurmountable debt and publicly declaring an opinion will definitely make you bankrupt. To avoid losing in the conversion, attempt converting anxiety into joy first whenever possible. That's the only true counter-currency—positive thinking—consistently thwarting illogical, circular thinking with positive, reinforcing thought. Since anxiety has high inflation, sometimes positive thoughts will feel like they are impossible to earn, ensuring, once again, the victory of anxiety.

Let me walk you through the math in more detail.
These sentences I am writing have to break through many negative thoughts just decorate the blank screen.

Every simple word feels like a triumph. That excitement reinforces my overall capacity for joy (positivity) and suddenly a whole sentence is out. Then a paragraph.

Anxiety will come collect later though, usually by isolating me from my friends and loved ones for at least 20 minutes, so that I can truly stew in my fear. I'll mark all of the things that still don't meet my ever-high standard. Noted adjectives that I could have made more colorful will add another 5 minutes to the debt. Misspelling a word and not catching it in spellcheck will undoubtedly evoke a memory of my mother telling me that I will unlikely be able to ever amount to anything worthwhile.

How about a scenario where the conversation is taking place face-to-face? I can't possibly enjoy friendly banter. That will send me to jail.

In addition, my anxiety market's gold standard is determined and reinforced by post-traumatic stress disorder. Having a flashback might buy me 14 minutes of reassurance from loved ones that I'm are alright. That's enough of a return, right? Since after each flashback there is a period of reacquainting myself with actual surroundings, i.e. reminding myself that I am not longer in said flashback, I get another 14 minutes to spend appreciating things like breathing instead of hyperventilating.

It's a sale. My brain will also throw-in the affirmation that my mother's past words no longer affect me as an adult. *You're welcome,* it says, like I'm getting the better end of the deal.

Other things cost **moments of my life I will never get back**, and I remember them all. I think of one and anxiety is sure to send them all swirling back: The job I kept because I didn't believe I could get a better one. The relationship I stayed in, even though I know I was not in love. The home I remained in because I was hoping things would get better. Anxiety is sure to remind me to really mull these over and feel bad that there is nothing I can change now.

So yeah, I can get 100 words, 10 minutes of peaceful writing time. For that I will pay in editing. *Everything is stupid and why do you even think anyone will read this*, says anxiety. The twentieth re-write still isn't good enough, so I quit writing, although it's all I ever wanted to do.

So, where does that leave me? Here's the final math: all of this will result in about 2 minutes of a reader's time. 3, if I'm lucky and something makes them read to the end.

Anxiety is exhausting. It feels like doing algebra blindfolded while riding a horse. It's like trying to understand the stock market, only to lose all your money when you finally have the bravery to get in.

No, there is no real conversion rate. But having one would make having anxiety so much easier. Imagine you knew how many good things will happen in your life if you just worry a certain amount? But anxiety doesn't work that way. In truth, all worrying creates, is **inaction**.

Now pardon me, I need to re-read and edit this at least five more times. Hopefully I can make it worth 5 minutes of your time, even though it will cost me at least 20 minutes of self-deprecation later.

21 Rejections

TWENTY-ONE REJECTIONS. Twenty-one times I questioned my worth, questioned why I couldn't produce something that was worthwhile for someone to approve. Twenty-one times I asked myself if it was worth it to keep going and whether I would ever achieve anything again. Twenty-one was the combination of four panels, four book pitches, one twitch partner application, and twelve article pitches to major outlets (two of which I actually had to write out completely) all in varied order. Actually, there were more, but these are the ones that graced me with a rejection notification.

After the first three, I felt like I had to keep going. It's a game of numbers, after all, I thought. The more I try, the more likely something will come back positive. Four more rolled in and I started to feel down. I re-evaluated what I had written up until that point to see where I could improve. I asked others to read through my content to see if I could make changes.

All the while that voice internally kept gaining volume. Telling me that no one would ever accept anything I did ever again. That my past successes were all flukes: that I either lucked out before or was accepted out of pity. Slowly, this voice grew louder and around pitch 12, I began listening to its unforgiving words even as I continued applying. I was giving up before I started. Some things went out without being proofread. I denied the help of others, no matter how unfair it was for me to disregard their genuine support and my time.

I quit counting the number of rejections for a bit as the wave of disappointment crashed into me. My creativity dying along with my hope. Each rejection became a hit against my existence, a tally of my flaws. Once a few more collected, I began to feel like I would never be successful again. I thought, of course, I was a failure and now everyone can see it. I felt like I was being put back into place, where I was used to being, where it was dark and lonely. But the thing is, I was hanging my worth on so many circumstances that I had no control over.

Rejections happen for all sorts of reasons: wrong time, someone already wrote something similar, the editor is in a bad mood, someone is biased against people with your background, and too many more to list.

Truth is: most of them have very little to do with you.

A rejection of something you made, is not a rejection of you as a person. It's a rejection of that particular thing at that particular time. Maybe your work wasn't accepted but that does not, in any way, reflect your worth.

You are a collection of every single piece of your being. Your body, your mind, your kind deeds, your caring attitude toward others, things you accomplished throughout your life. A rejection in a moment, cannot define us.

Now I realize I should not have kept pushing myself when I already felt defeated. I should not have punished myself over what others thought, over something I had so little control over.

When I tune out that dreadful voice, I know deep down that I did the best I could with the resources and knowledge I had in that moment. Accepting those rejections as constructive feedback of my work means that I will continue to grow and what I create will ultimately get better.

Our lives will be full of accomplishments and disappointments. They will be full of laughter and tears. Assuming that everything needs to be a victory dulls the color of those moments when we are successful. It takes away our ability to enjoy the journey we are on. Accepting, and maybe even embracing, that not everything I do or make will receive approval might not be easy, but leaves room for me to show myself more grace and kindness. It leaves room for me to be human. So after this last series of rejections, I have come to realize that in order to produce my best work, I must first accept myself as a work in progress.

The Beauty of Every Moment of Recovery from Depression

CLIMBING OUT A DEPRESSION can be excruciating. I often feel physical pain on top of the emotional anguish. The combination can keep me down for weeks at a time. When I am in the very dark depths of such feelings, even getting to the surface or high enough to witness the light outside feels insurmountable.

In these moments, as I attempt to get out of bed, I imagine an alternate version of myself. One that is out, maybe shopping or socializing with a friend. I imagine that person receiving love, but instead of feeling motivated to move toward that image, I grow jealous. In the present, I feel no love for myself, everything is dark and bleak and hopeless -- a stark contrast to my alternate-reality self.

But if I stop for a moment, and think about what my good days are like, I remember that it's not as though life becomes perfect in the days where I can function fully. On days when I am not depressed, I am not automatically going to make my way to an amusement park, or go on vacation to a new city, or do anything else I find to be fun and thrilling. Most of those good days I will be at work in the office, or at home doing laundry trying to take advantage of finally being in a good headspace. Is this important to my life? Yes. Is it thrilling and exhilarating? No.

But I am so used to expecting only incredible, exciting things from myself, that the lack thereof can on its own can feel depressing at times. Looking at everyone else's highlight reels on social media, in movies or TV, it's easy to think that I am not doing enough to make my life exciting.

It's as though I imagine my "better" self to be so idyllic as a way to continue to put myself further down into the cave of despair. To tell myself, "See, if only you could be less depressed, you could be having the best life." But that "best life" doesn't exist. It's just life.

And being able to appreciate all of the small moments when I feel well, usually leaves me feeling so much better than when I am dwelling on the moments I feel like I should be having.

What does this entail? That means expressing gratitude to myself when I feel well. It means taking a moment while I am folding laundry to praise myself for doing a chore, when I know there are more exciting things to do.

What's more important, is actively participating in life by experiencing the moments, dull and exciting alike. Which require work and effort, no matter how many or few illnesses someone might have. It requires work to keep up friendships, continuously stay in touch, and care for others. And appreciating yourself for all of the work you do on seemingly mundane things means creating positive, encouraging feedback to myself. Which in turn incentivizes me to do more and be kinder to myself.

Eventually, with enough of this positive feedback, I have started to feel less inclined to expect a linear recovery with rainbows and ice cream at every bend. Instead I want to feel all of the dull good days and the dull bad days because they are part of my journey as a whole. And that journey overall, having the chance to be part of it at all, is exhilarating.

The Bastardization Of Positive Psychology: Recasting negative experiences isn't the same thing as blind optimism

ABOUT 10 YEARS AGO, my sister sent me a link to psychologist Martin Seligman's TED Talk. Seligman's life's work in positive psychology has been distilled by pop culture enough that I was seething when I saw the link. *Thank you,* I thought, *another schmuck telling me to look at the bright side of things when I want to die. Sure, I will just look for the positive in life and be cured.*

After doing some research, though, I recognize the nuances Seligman couldn't explore in 20 minutes. Those nuances unravel an entire physiological philosophy that can actually help many people lead more productive lives.

Positive psychology is defined as "the scientific study of the strengths that enable individuals and communities to thrive." The idea came about when Seligman and his colleagues wanted to address how negative the relatively new science of psychology had been, as it focused heavily on pathologizing and addressing wrong behaviors.

Instead, Seligman noted in his practice that it was always beneficial to create more productive environments, focusing attention away from the pain and into things that help enhance positive emotions.

So, if psychology was about finding problems that needed repair, positive psychology theorized that it would be more productive to instead find what drives us and shift our attention to that.

Unfortunately, this nuanced version is not how most people seem to understand positive psychology. Armed with its pop-philosophy variant, some fashion and lifestyle bloggers are pushing the positivity concept to a limiting point, distilling it to extreme optimism:

> Focus on the good in life only, always look for the bright side, and be grateful for what you have instead of thinking about what you don't. Remove anyone who does not agree with this, as they are negative.

...or something close to that.

Those actions just further perpetuate the myth that if you work hard enough, your life can be picture perfect.

I have seen posts about poor mental health deleted from comment sections on the basis that it brought the conversation down. Such actions just further perpetuate the myth that if you work hard enough, your life can be picture perfect — which, by extension, means depression is just a manifestation of someone not trying hard enough to be happy. Worse, instead of this elusive joy that so many social media influencers talk about in sterilized, slightly vague terms, our time on social media is more likely to make us feel worse because of the comparison it automatically cultivates.

After over 15 years of positive psychology permeating culture, it's not the positivity that makes us cringe and feel awful—it's feeling forced to compare our mundane to someone else's appearance of constant joy. Our self-esteem feels threatened when we think we might be someone else's downward comparison (when you compare yourself to someone doing worse than you are). You might feel the urge to double down and say, "I just need to focus on being happy more, work harder." But is that really the answer?

If someone is experiencing clinical depression and is in a general cathartic state, positivity is not something that can be comprehended. If you think the only path to happiness is feeling positive, yet you are incapable of feeling that way because of mental illness, you're defeated before you've even begun.

I cannot emphasize enough that this was far from the original intention of positive psychology. The textbook version of positive psychology is noticing those encounters that normally make us feel awful about ourselves and learning how to see them in a brighter light. It's not an objective rejection of reality or brushing things under the rug; it's reteaching our minds to look for the best instead of the worst in any situation.

Few people know that Seligman came up with positive psychology while seeking to understand depression and other mental illnesses. He observed that people who experience the same event may end up describing it in a variety of ways depending on their general outlook of life, and those who were able to look at things in a positive light were less likely to be depressed.

It's not that the theory is unhelpful, it's that for those dealing with depression, imagining another thinking pattern or having control over the chemicals in their brains is impossible. And this improper interpretation of Seligman's idea can create even more social pressure for people with depression.

There is so much more to life than just smiling for a camera or posting a picture of your meal. There are nuances that get missed when we focus on only sharing pleasure. Deleting someone's comment about their struggles perpetuates this idea that we need to bottle up and deny our negative emotions. Not only is that a diversion from actual positive psychology, it can be deeply damaging for people who need support the most.

Writer's block. Mental block.

I CAN'T WRITE. All of my writing is either bad or doesn't deserve to be read. it doesn't matter that I have been published by major media outlets. It doesn't matter that I have received compliments. All the times someone has told me my writing was awful echo so much louder than kind words do.

Although I know that any unsolicited feedback is more telling of the commenter than it is useful, it sits at the forefront of my mind every time I open my laptop. I begin beating myself up when I am already vulnerable, in the midst of asking myself to pour my thoughts out. And yet, I still expect myself to just start. To do so without taking the time to put myself back together first.

I do put in an effort to get myself into the right state of mind. I have a ritual. I sit down, cover myself with blankets, which then prompts my dog to cozy up to me. I stare at the screen, re-read my favorite Steve Martin essay, put on music, maybe a comforting show on TV, yet it's all too often still not enough.

I might start typing, but once a sentence goes wrong (maybe I messed up the structure), I am instantly brought back to the time when, after applying for a writing job, the editor wrote back "There are two kinds of writing skill issues out there. One I can teach (spelling, etc), and another I can't. Your issues are something that I can't help with."

I should think about the time when Medium named me a Top Writer in Mental Health. Instead, I am fixated on the moment I noticed that the title was removed. I thought I had gotten over it until it's time to write a new piece, and suddenly it's a new wound again.

It doesn't help that sometimes the compliments hurt and make me feel ungrateful. "That piece really made me think," or "but I love your writing" — are just like tennis balls for the mind to beat back. I just counter with "they just don't want me to feel sad," or "now how can I write something half as good as that other thing was." People might commend me for writing so consistently, something which you think is inarguable. But I respond internally, "actually it feels like a small cage I chose to get into and then asked someone to hide the key."

The thoughts are so belligerent they make me stop, if for no other reason, but because it might make the noise end. I turn off the music, turn the TV to mute — and nothing. Just a blinking cursor. I turn off the TV, get up and pace, do some breathing exercises, some jumping jacks, then sit down and google "avoiding writer's block." Before I know it, instead I am just lost in the cloud of the internet.

It's a conundrum. When you tell your brain: "Don't think about the lemon. No lemon, no lemon thoughts," all you can see is yellow citrus. But should I tell myself: "Write, writing, wrote" — all I can think of is how bad I am at it. The transitive property just doesn't work for some reason.

The negative thoughts have a way of sneaking their way in, they don't have to work hard to win my attention over everything else. Once they've found their roots, it will take some tools to rip them out. First, you have to find something to remind you that your thoughts are not correct. That what you believe is not actually the truth.

The way I eventually prove them wrong is by simply doing what I meant to do. I start.

Here's how. You give the ugly, obstructive, planted idea of self-doubt a good tug. Disagree with it. Prove it wrong with action. If it doesn't budge, you stop for a moment because the mental labor has made you exhausted. Then you notice the light behind the plant. The light coming from an idea so bright and warm, you crave to feel it. You resolve to tug again. You finally unearth the ugly creature.

For a few hours, maybe days, hopefully, weeks, you see things clearly and unobstructed. Always some spores remain in the ground though. Slowly, we start the cycle all over again.

So yeah, sometimes I am a bad writer, but maybe it's not because I am a bad writer, but rather, because I am bad at giving myself permission to fail.

Exclusive Essay for *Well That Explains It*

Why the World Needs More Empaths

I LAY IN BED TURNED TO THE WALL, studying it intensely, praying to myself that one of two things will happen: either I just disappear from the world, or I find the energy to get out of bed. As I lay there admonishing myself for being lazy, unmotivated and incapable of doing such a basic task, there is a knock on the door. Without pause, the door opens and my father bursts in.

"Well, how long are you going to lay in bed for?"
"I don't feel well," I reply.
"What, you have a fever?"
"No, I just can't get up."

His tone becomes serious, commanding: "Alright, enough of this, I don't want to hear it. You have five minutes to get up." And as he closes the door behind himself, I hear him additionally mumble: "This again."

I don't blame anyone who has a hard time when they know their loved one is depressed. I do have a problem when someone is clearly aware the other person is hurt, but is so adamant about not having to confront someone else's pain, that they ask the person hurting to ignore their own needs, to push them down. It baffles me that someone can be empathetic enough to be aware that someone appears to be in pain, but so apathetic as to not even offer sympathy.

No matter how often they get used interchangeably, *empathy* and *sympathy* are not one in the same. Empathy requires emotional investment, placing oneself into someone's metaphorical else's shoes. It's about relating to another person through one's emotions.

Sympathy, on the other hand, does not go past the surface of relating to one's own feelings. It's the difference between grieving with someone when their loved one dies as you can almost feel their pain and offering them your condolences because you can acknowledge that grief is known to be a sad emotion.

I grew up craving empathy from others, while having an excess of it myself. I studied TV shows, movies and every other piece of media, watching characters and their interactions. Watching their reactions to situations taught me how to relate to other people. I would put myself in their shoes as a way to better understand how interpersonal relationships worked, because I felt that at home, my parents were not responding to me in a matter than reflected what I saw culturally around me. The result was that I consistently began to put myself into another's shoes, no matter whether the situation called for it.

I recall reading *Harry Potter* and really getting upset when his life was in danger. Or anxious to the point that my stomach turned as he took Polyjuice Potion to impersonate an enemy. It wasn't until recently, in my early twenties, that I recognized that perhaps I was too good at understanding another person's emotions and relating to them, as every experience outside of me was consistently felt strongly on the inside too. I can't watch one of those Animal Protection commercials without crying because I felt the dog in the pound must feel sad and lonely.

People who feel this way, are commonly referred to as empaths (psychic telepath): someone who experiences other people's emotions as strongly as they experience their own. The word was first used in this form in a 1956 Science

Fiction novel and made popular by what else? *Star Trek* in the 1970s.

Sometimes empathy is so consuming that one might think as though they can actually feel exactly what another is going through. This is the fallacy of an empath, no matter how closely we understand what someone might be going through, no matter how similar our experiences, we are not actually that person and therefore cannot assume we fully understand how they experience the world. That gap is closed by sympathy. The parts that we cannot grasp because they are separate experiences, we can sympathize with.

We need empathy to talk about mental health because things like depression and anxiety don't make sense and are not too easy to comprehend otherwise. They're often nonsensical. Like someone experiencing anhedonia on their wedding day because of their depression. Or someone feeling a sense of dread so strong that they fear and avoid amusement parks altogether, due to their anxiety about germs. Whereas a neurotypical person might be able to walk away and just wash their hands one more extra time.

According to TakeThis.org's Mental Health Ambassador training, empathy as one of the four major steps in helping someone experiencing a mental health issue. When someone is feeling unwell mentally, a great way to connect is to tell them how you believe you may feel if you were in their shoes.

Saying "that must hurt a lot," when someone stubs their toe on the side of the bed is a lot more emotionally connecting than saying, "sorry you stubbed your foot." If it's part of the process of mental health first aide, it must be crucial in continuing conversations towards good mental health.

The central issue is that all of this is lacking at the core of the social stigma we still see with understanding mental health. I feel discussions around the subject are few and far between outside of the mental health support communities that have sprouted up online. There are of course the usual suspected culprits for this current lack of empathy: video games, social media and news coverage.

I disagree. I think that video games are another medium for us to experience emotional journeys of characters and social media (as mentioned above) does a lot to connect people with the support systems they need across the world.

I believe the actual issue lies in the sheer number of people and related information we consume daily. We just don't have the bandwidth emotionally to care more.

As an example, according to psychologists, charitable giving is largely successful when the consumer can empathize with the cause. One way to do so, is to ensure that only one person is featured in the ad. This is because we are easily able to relate to one human. Seeing too many people, or even cold hard statistics on why the cause is important makes us feel like the problem is impersonal and makes us less likely to give.

In the same vein, we can only socially care for so many people at once. According to anthropologist Robin Dunbar's research, that number is about 150 at any given time. But between every person we are connected with online and how accessible everyone is at any given moment, from people at work to long lost relatives we still get to keep up with on Facebook, it's difficult to connect with everyone without exhausting ourselves. Which is why many prefer not to. Sympathy is the next best thing we got, but it's not enough.

My father and I would have had a very different relationship were he able to react in an empathetic way when he heard I was unwell. For someone with a healthy psyche, seeing someone say they are just not motivated to get up might cause frustration, thinking how they themselves were able to just push through instead of staying in bed.

Had he instead thought about my character and how bubbly and happy to get up out of bed I normally was, putting himself into my mindset normally, he may have been able to empathize with how deep my pain must have been to not even want to get up.

Sympathy is saying, I hope that stops. Apathy is saying, I need you to make this stop. Empathy is saying, how can we get this to stop together? In a solution-oriented, work-driven world, we are too exhausted to care, and it shows. But we won't be able to have productive conversations about mental health until things reverse.

Bonus Memoir Preview

Oh My Creep: A Christmas Story

WE PRETENDED TO BE A TYPICAL American family every Christmas. My mother, having bought all of the decorations and toys during the previous year's sale, would go all out decorating the house. Her strangely overzealous attempts were meant to assure everyone around that she was patriotic.

My mother and sister led me to believe that our Russian-American house was special and various Santa-figures visited throughout the month of December. First, Santa would come and bring the tree, then he would come back to bring presents for Christmas and finally on New Year's Day, his Russian cousin Ded Moroz [Grandpa Frost] would bring small, stocking-stuffer-type gifts. That's three times the excitement for you folks counting at home. And three times I would be sent to bed early. I would lay there, unable to sleep while my parents assembled our 7-foot tree. I believed and I never complained.

The problem was the next morning after the tree set up, when my mother would finish by adding her favorite, creepy animatronic toys underneath. Knowing these were not Santa's fault, I did not hesitate to stare at the toys as they moved, hoping to set them on fire a la *Matilda* and her dad's television.

From left to right under the tree were: a tiny, harmless light up model house, a Mickey Mouse dressed as Santa motioning with a candy cane in hand, and a young girl with a present in one hand and a candle in another. But it wasn't the eerie head-bopping Mickey, or the little girl with the crystal eyes that gave me the worst case of the heebie jeebies.

On the far right under the tree stood a Santa, who moved his head back and forth to an infinite musical loop, exclaimed "Oh My Feet" and left me wondering why the old man would allow a likeliness of himself to look so crappy.

If nothing else, this representation made no sense. First, Santa would never complain about the cold because

a—He lived in the North Pole where it's not exactly like Hawaii and

b—He is obviously magical and no magical being needs a hot water tub to make himself feel better.

If Santa were to freeze his feet while walking around, apparently collecting letters in his satchel, why would he sit down to an empty tub to warm them up? I found a video of the creep online[101] for demonstration, but I don't recommend watching it before bedtime. I had to unwrap my presents in front of him, while he looked at me like he was about to steal my soul. If nothing else, he had that look in his eyes…

Of course, my mom found this Satan (see what I did there?) toy to be endlessly amusing, and even made sure that he took the trip to Russia when she put together the storage container. I don't know where the bastard is now, but I'll do anything to ensure he never finds his way into any home of mine again.

---

[101] *https://www.youtube.com/watch?v=zwlZr53Zxsg*

"**IF YOU REALLY WANTED THIS,** you would find the motivation and just do it! I don't want to hear any more about how you're having a hard time. If you want to do it, just do it."

The voice on the line was stern and had lost their temper. In exchange for helping them with their social media, a life coach had agreed to give me a few sessions of their time. I had just finished telling them that I was having a hard time feeling like anything I wrote would be worthwhile and that was their response. We didn't speak ever again but their words echoed in my mind for a very long time.

It's not like I had an easy time writing before, but now the mere idea of writing down something I was thinking felt audacious. Who the hell told me that I could have an opinion? Who said that my writing was worth presenting onto a page? Then, in early 2016, my husband told me about a co-worker of his was part of a writing group and would be willing to spell check and generally edit something if I wrote it. Which, after my poor attempt to create a website in 2013, it was obvious that was something I clearly needed.

At the time, I used to sit at home in the evenings with an open laptop and just cry. I couldn't get myself to put down words onto a page. I just couldn't. I vaguely knew the coworker my husband was talking about, having met him at a Christmas party beforehand. He seemed like a nice guy, but I was so certain that my writing was so atrocious that he would recoil at the idea once he read even just one of my pieces.

About two months later, I finally talked to this co-worker. Then it took me another two weeks to produce a 1000 word piece for him to check out. Meanwhile, I thoroughly enjoyed reading samples of his writing that he over for me to review in exchange. I remember thinking: *Well this is writing, not like what my shit is.*

Then my writing came back to me. It was just as awful as I thought. The document was bleeding red. And I felt an immense sense of... relief. The edits were all constructive, with suggestions on how to improve everything instead of just ruling the pieces out totally. So, then I sat down and wrote another piece. And another. Sure, they were months in between, but I was writing. All it took was one person who was productive in their criticism and suddenly it felt like I wasn't just a ball of slime, I felt like I could finally do what I always dreamed of doing, since I wrote those poems as a seven year old.

What I want to say the most is thank you. Thank you for every word you read. Thank you for helping give my words purpose and meaning. From the first comment of encouragement I ever received on Medium to Sarah Fader, who messaged me and said "it would be stupid not to" when I second-guessed the need to publish this compilation of work—making it a real freakin' book. To every person who ever told me that my words had meaning. Thank you.

Thanks

Special thanks go out to Sarah Fader and the whole team who helped give my words a loving home.

Huge thank you to the Shanleys: You finally made me understand what a family is when you accepted me into yours.

This book would have never existed without every proofreader and editor who has helped shape my writing in the past two years. How can I ever repay you: Endre, Patrick (PainPK0), and Dylan (0ptimysticgamer).

Endre—you taught me to believe in my own writing. Without you, Mxiety would have never existed.

Dr. P, how many sessions did I sit there and say, "I just wish I could write something." And how many times did you promise me I would? Thank you for teaching me to accept my mental health. Dare I say, without you, I wouldn't truly know the meaning of those two words.

Some people in the live streaming space have done so much to encourage me to keep going and I will be forever grateful for their incredible support: Raffael (TheeDrB), Rachel (DrKowert) [and all of the TakeThis org], Ceddy (GreenDumpling), Cassey (Videogamediva), Vanessa (Gothix), Jessy (JessyQuil), Candace (VampireKitten), AshniChrist, Asikaa, Akirakietsu, Rudy Caseres (and the rest of the SPSM gang), and my livestream moderators: Serene, Tracer, Bryce, Tali, Jinx, Bliffle, Dawnstar.

And to every single person who believes in what I am trying to do. Thank you!

About the Author:

Marie Shanley is better known as Mxiety online, a live talk show host, conversationalist and writer. Marie lives with her husband and adorable corgi, Flynn, in Northern New Jersey. There she drinks tea and overthinks everything she puts on paper, hoping that her words help someone out there in the real world. Her goal is to solve the mental health crisis by bridging the gap between mental health professionals and those living with mental illnesses.

You can find her @Mxiety on Twitter, Mixer, Youtube, Patreon, Instagram and Twitch, and continue to keep up with her blogs @ mxiety.com

www.ingramcontent.com/pod-product-compliance
Lightning Source LLC
Chambersburg PA
CBHW051545020426
42333CB00016B/2107